# BFI Modern Classics

**Rob White**
Series Editor

Advancing into its second century, the cinema as a mature art form with an established list of classics. But contemporary cinema is so subject to every shift in fashion regarding aesthetics, morals and ideas that judgments on the true worth of recent films are liable to be risky and controversial; yet they are essential if we want to know where the cinema is going and what it can achieve.

As part of the British Film Institute's commitment to the promotion and evaluation of contemporary cinema, and in conjunction with the influential BFI Film Classics series, BFI Modern Classics is a series of books devoted to individual films of recent years. Distinguished film critics, scholars and novelists explore the production and reception of their chosen films in the context of an argument about the film's quality and importance. Insightful, considered, often impassioned, these elegant, well-illustrated books will set the agenda for debates about what matters in modern cinema.

BFI MODERN CLASSICS

# The Right Stuff

**Tom Charity**

BFI PUBLISHING

First published in 1997 by the
**British Film Institute**
21 Stephen Street, London W1P 2LN

Copyright © Tom Charity 1997

The British Film Institute exists to promote
appreciation, enjoyment, protection and
development of moving image culture in and
throughout the whole of the United Kingdom.
Its activities include the National Film and
Television Archive; the National Film Theatre;
the Museum of the Moving Image;
the London Film Festival; the production and
distribution of film and video; funding and
support for regional activities; Library and
Information Services; Stills, Posters and
Designs; Research; Publishing and Education;
and the monthly *Sight and Sound* magazine.

Designed by Andrew Barron &
Collis Clements Associates

Typeset in Garamond Simoncini
by Fakenham Photosetting Ltd

Picture editing by Millie Simpson

Printed in Great Britain

British Library Cataloguing-in-Publication Data
A catalogue record for this book is available
from the British Library
ISBN 0-85170-624-X

# Contents

## Dedication

**For Fiona**

# Acknowledgments

This manuscript wouldn't have made it but for the interest, support, advice and encouragement of a good many friends and colleagues. My deepest thanks to Geoff Andrew, who is both, and who offered all of the above and more. Thanks to Rob White and Ed Buscombe, my editors at the BFI, to David Thomson, Kent Jones and Orapin Tantimedh at Cappa Productions for invaluable access to tapes, to Trevor Johnston, especially for his comments on the score, to Sorley Macdonald and Geoffrey Macnab for their generous assistance, to Rob Stone, Dominic Wells, Wally Hammond and Derek Adams, Brian Case, and – always – Fiona Morrow. I must cite Spiro Kyriacou's unpublished thesis 'The nostalgia for futurism in *The Right Stuff*' as another useful source. I am grateful to Irwin Winkler and Scott Glenn for their reminiscences, and, most especially, to Philip Kaufman, who made himself available to me and donated supplementary materials. All unattributed quotations from Kaufman in the book derive from our conversations.

Picture credits. All pictures from BFI stills, posters and designs except: Frank Spooner (pp. 3, 18, 63, 66, 67, 71, 87); Philip Kaufman (pp. 9, 28, 52); Ronald Grant (pp. 15, 46–7); Moviestore (p. 42). All stills from *The Right Stuff* courtesy The Ladd Co.

# Introduction

*The Right Stuff* is a return to the roots of the Western. It was made in answer
to the question: 'What happened to the Western?' *Philip Kaufman*[1]

The Western is the quintessential American genre, where white America
grapples with its character, its conscience and its sense of self. The
Western affords America an heroic vision of its history and heritage, a
mythology to call its own. It romanticises the pioneer and eulogises the
wilderness. It negotiates the ambivalent terrain between law and anarchy,
social responsibility and individual freedom, stasis and flux. Its trajectory
is inevitably towards obsolescence: by the time the Western became
established, the West was all over bar the shouting, and as the genre
matured, 'progress' had begun to sound like a dirty word. It is the purest
form of movie, the starkest and most physical of philosophical dramas.
It is prone to announce itself with an iconic rider against the landscape,
and often ends the same way. It is a very masculine genre, trading on
fantasies of absolute male autonomy, dexterity and moral imperative.
It is fundamentally concerned with the construction of the hero.

 *The Right Stuff* is not a Western exactly, but it is very definitely a
film about pioneer mythology, the changing light of history and the
nature of heroism in modern America. Hailing an 'instant classic', the
American reviewers must have jinxed it, for this big-budget epic flopped
at the box-office and has never recovered its lustre. Something of a
media phenomenon on its release (featured on the cover of *Newsweek*
on down), the film has scarcely been written about since, enjoying little
of the rich cultural afterlife associated with analogous titles such as
*Apocalypse Now*, *Raging Bull* or even *Heaven's Gate*. *The Right Stuff*
is too idiosyncratic a picture to fit neatly into larger theoretical
frameworks. A hip movie about 'square' subjects (astronauts, the
military, courage, patriotism), it ranges freely across apparently
contradictory styles: mythic and satiric, documentary and surreal, even
epic and underground. An auteur's film, written and directed by Philip

Kaufman, it is nevertheless dictated by history and faithful to Tom Wolfe's chronicle of that history, the bestseller on which it is based. These are some of the tensions which make *The Right Stuff* so fascinating, and which I wanted to explore in this book. It is a book about the permutation of history: about America in the 50s and the children of that time, their heroes and dreams, the world they found when they grew up, and the movies they made to make sense of the disparity.

Kids like to try on many different hats, to see which ones fit. Perhaps I watched too many films as a boy. I wanted to be a cowboy and an astronaut. Then, when I was a little older, I thought I should become an actor so that I could wear all the hats I wanted. I never got much further than the mirror in that regard – the other side of the cinema screen – but such flights of fantasy may be where this book came from.

(Above) Sam Shepard looks on as Philip Kaufman explains a point
(Overleaf) Sam Shepard and General Charles Yeager

# 1 The Space Race: 1957–63

Together let us explore the stars
*John F. Kennedy*, Inaugural Address, 20 January 1961

12 April 1961: man orbits the earth for the first time. 'The space age has begun,' declared American astronaut John Glenn, swallowing his disappointment. A twenty-seven-year-old test pilot called Yuri Gagarin had beaten him to it. The Soviets made off with the first prize in what was designated the 'space race', a mysterious adjunct to the nuclear arms race which held a powerful grip on the imagination of the global powers. Space technology carried a real threat: if the Soviets could propel Sputnik beyond the earth's atmosphere, even put satellites into orbit above American air space, then nowhere was safe from nuclear attack. (Just weeks after Gagarin's flight, America woke up to another missile crisis, in Cuba.) But there was more to America's fascination with space than this: popular culture's obsession with science fiction and science speculation, space travel, UFOs and alien life forms (confusingly aligned with Communism in the psyche of 50s Hollywood B-movies) had something to do with it, and behind that, aeons under the cosmic sway of the sun and the moon. Space was the last great unknown, John Kennedy's 'new frontier', the place where science and superstition merged.

President Eisenhower instigated Project Mercury on 7 October 1958, one year and three days after the Soviets had successfully launched Sputnik 1 into orbit. Speaking as the Senate majority leader, Lyndon Baines Johnson talked about the need to control the 'high ground' of space: 'The Roman Empire controlled the world because it could build roads. Later – when it moved to sea – the British Empire was dominant because it had ships. In the air age we were powerful because we had airplanes. Now the Communists have established a foothold in outer space.' John McCormack, the head of the House Select Committee on Astronautics, was even more graphic. The US faced 'national extinction', he said. 'It cannot be over-emphasised that the survival of the free world – indeed, all the world – is caught up in the stakes.'[2]

Not only were the Soviets winning the race, but the US was struggling to get off the ground at all. In December 1957, the first televised countdown to a US satellite launch had ended humiliatingly with the mighty Vanguard rocket lifting off just six inches before crumpling into a ball of smoke and flame. Project Mercury was first and foremost about salvaging national pride. It wasn't entrusted to the Navy or the Air Force, but to the National Advisory Committee for Aeronautics, henceforth known as the National Aeronautics and Space Administration – NASA.

According to NASA's own project review published in October 1963, Mercury had three basic objectives: '(1) Place a manned

spacecraft in orbital flight around the earth. (2) Investigate man's performance capabilities and his ability to function in the environment of space. (3) Recover the man and spacecraft safely.'[3]

The Mercury Seven as portrayed in *The Right Stuff* (from top left: Alan Shepard, John Glenn, Gordo Cooper, Gus Grissom, Deke Slayton, Wally Schirra and Scott Carpenter)

Mercury was modified from a plan known as MISS – Man in Space Soonest. This wasn't a forward-looking, coherent strategy to rationalise the US space programme so much as a political quick-fix, a scramble to make ground in a Cold War PR fiasco. The rocket scientists weren't happy. To them, the astronaut was a 'redundant component', fit only for bio-medical research. The pilots (Eisenhower insisted that the astronauts should be military test pilots) weren't happy either. They were already reaching the outer limits of the atmosphere in their experimental X-1 rocket planes. The space capsules envisaged by NASA were comparatively crude and couldn't be piloted in any meaningful way. The astronaut was a passenger. A guinea pig.

Project Mercury ran for four-and-a-half years and accomplished six successful manned space flights in a 25-flight programme, but it came to only one fundamental scientific conclusion: 'that man can function ably as a pilot-engineer-experimenter without undesirable reactions or deteriorations of normal body functions for periods up to 34 hours of weightless flight'.[4] NASA estimated that more than two million people contributed to the programme. Of these, seven became momentarily the most famous men in America.

## 2 The Write Stuff: 1959–79

On 9 April 1959 in Washington, the press were introduced to the seven volunteers selected to become the Mercury astronauts. John Glenn, Alan Shepard, Gordo Cooper, Gus Grissom, Deke Slayton, Wally Schirra and Scott Carpenter were all distinguished pilots, if by no means America's finest. They were all graduates in engineering. They were slightly shorter than the national average (Mercury could only accommodate astronauts up to 1.8 metres tall), but they were otherwise the very embodiment of what America liked to see when it looked in the mirror. They were all male and all white (though no one thought to comment on that then); they were church-going, and happily married, they said. Reporting on the press conference in the *New York Times*, journalist James Reston wrote:

The Seven in the offices of *Life* magazine (production still)

What made them so exciting was not that they said anything new but that they said all the old things with such fierce convictions ... They spoke of 'duty' and 'faith' and 'country' like Walt Whitman's pioneers ... This is a pretty cynical town, but nobody went away from these young men scoffing at their courage and idealism.[5]

Reston's view was typical. The next day's newspapers feted them as national heroes. By the summer, the seven men and their wives had signed an exclusive deal with *Life* magazine for their personal stories. The deal – worth $500,000 between them – kept the rest of an already compliant press at arm's length and ensured that only an officially sanctioned version of events appeared in print. When *Life* published a photograph of the seven wives, it airbrushed out every blemish.

Fifteen years on, when Tom Wolfe came to write the definitive chronicle of Project Mercury, he had no more interest in scoffing at the astronauts' courage than James Reston had. Courage was his subject, the astronauts his heroes. *The Right Stuff* is 'not interested in the exploration of space per se', he says in the foreword to the 1983 edition. 'What is it, I wondered, that makes a man willing to sit up on top of an enormous Roman candle, such as a Redstone, Atlas, Titan or Saturn rocket, and wait for someone to light the fuse?' Nevertheless, Wolfe had no truck with the complacent adulation he found in the cuttings files, reserving his severest scorn for 'the consummate hypocritical Victorian gent', that 'great colonial Animal', the American press. 'In the late 1950s ... the animal seemed determined that in all matters of national importance the *proper emotion*, the *seemly sentiment*, the *fitting moral tone* should be established ... the public, the populace, the citizenry, must be provided with *the correct feelings*!'

Tom Wolfe was born Thomas Kennerley in 1931 in Richmond, Virginia. After graduating from Yale with a doctorate in American Studies he became a reporter. 'Chicago, 1928, that was the general idea ... I wanted the whole movie, nothing left out.'[6] In 1962, he became a feature writer on *The New York Herald Tribune*. There, and in pieces for

*Esquire*, Wolfe established himself at the forefront of a movement which came to be called the 'New Journalism'. In an essay of the same name, published in 1973 with an anthology of pieces by the likes of Michael Herr, Terry Southern, Hunter S. Thompson, Norman Mailer, John Gregory Dunne and Joe Eszterhas, Wolfe argues that by concerning itself with the real world, with sociological context and precise, detailed reportage, the movement was the true heir to the novelistic tradition of the 19th century, to the great realists Balzac, Gogol and Dickens. If there was anything 'new' in the new journalism, he said, it was simply this: 'The discovery that it was possible to write accurate non-fiction with techniques usually associated with novels and short stories ... to use any literary device, from the traditional dialogisms of the essay to stream-of-consciousness, and to use many different kinds simultaneously.'[7]

The full title of the 1963 *Esquire* article which made Wolfe's name was 'There Goes (Varoom! Varoom!) That Kandy-Kolored (Thphhhhhh!) Tangerine-Flake Streamline Baby (Rahghhh!) Around the Bend (Brummmmmmmmmmmmmmmmmmmm) ...'. Wolfe's style caught the eye. That was the point. He used onomatopoeia, mimesis, even odd typography to disrupt the polite conventions of the form. His incantatory, souped-up, capitalised, italicised, impacted prose took reportage beyond factual description and into the realms of psychology and the emotions, and it put the writer centre-stage. But, he insisted, it was all based on plain, old-fashioned legwork. If he described a subject's state of mind through interior monologue, that wasn't imaginative fiction, it was based on in-depth interviews. 'Eventually, I, and others, would be accused of "entering people's minds",' he writes in *The New Journalism*: 'But exactly! I figured that was one more doorbell a reporter had to push.'[8] The result was a vivid, vital social commentary, both ironic and romantic, a swinging, shifting tone which caught the cultural cross-currents of the time.

Based on a series of articles written for *Rolling Stone* magazine in 1973, *The Right Stuff* proved an immediate bestseller when it was published in 1979. The critical reception was equally warm. The consensus was that, at last, the talented Mr Wolfe had hit upon an epic

Tom Wolfe

subject as rich and rewarding as his prose. Wolfe had talked to the astronauts and their families, he had access to NASA files, even transcripts of post-flight debriefings. In short, he had the inside story on Mercury. He also had a scoop – a bona fide four-star hero by the name of Chuck Yeager.

Wolfe had set out to lionise America's astronauts, to try to comprehend the psychology of a man who volunteers to sit on top of a rocket and take it to the moon – but the astronauts took him to Yeager instead. 'All but a few [of the astronauts] had been military test pilots ... and it was this that led me to a rich and fabulous terrain that, in a literary sense, had remained as dark as the far side of the moon for more than half a century: military flying and the modern American officer corps.'9 Wolfe discovered that a career Navy pilot faced a twenty-three per cent chance of dying in an accident – a figure that didn't even include combat deaths (which were not regarded as 'accidental' in Navy statistics). If courage can be measured in the odds, then this was bravery above and beyond the call of any received notions of duty. In one thirty-six week period at Edwards Air Force Base in 1952, sixty-two Air Force pilots died. What kind of morale could sustain such losses? When Wolfe found Yeager, he began to piece together an answer none of the pilots would ever articulate.

Yeager was the ace of aces. He grew up in the West Virginia coalfields but enlisted in the Air Force in 1941 at the age of eighteen. On 12 October 1944 he shot down five German planes in one day. By the time he was twenty-two, he had thirteen-and-a-half kills, and when the war ended, the Air Force sent him to Muroc Field (later renamed Edwards) in California to test the XS-1 rocket planes. On 14 October 1947 Yeager broke the sound barrier. Reaching a speed of Mach 1.05, he became the fastest man in history – only the Air Force didn't tell anybody about it. (In 1952 Yeager suffered the indignity of attending the US premiere of David Lean's *The Sound Barrier*, which imaginatively bestowed the glory on a Brit.) By the time the security clearances had been sorted out, the record was old news. Another pilot, Scott

Crossfield, made some noise when he broke Mach 2 in 1953, and Yeager felt compelled to make it Mach 2.4 three weeks later. But when NASA started recruiting astronauts five years after that, Yeager wouldn't even have qualified – he hadn't been to college. In any case he wouldn't have applied. As late as 1983, General Yeager was telling *Interview* magazine that the government had backed the wrong horse in 1958:

Research is done for a purpose, and that is to get data that we can apply to weapons systems. When we worked ourselves to the edge of space starting with airplanes like the X-1 … that was a stepping stone to space. The natural evolution would have been to carry on the same technique … the decision was made, and it's not up to me to question that decision. But now it's obvious that decision was wrong.[10]

With his unparalleled flying record, laconic bravado and independent streak, Yeager struck Wolfe as the natural hero of his book. He had broken the sound barrier, but quietly – and, as Wolfe discovered, with two busted ribs. Wolfe was nothing if not style-conscious, and Yeager had style in spades. If he hadn't already bestowed the garland on demolition derby driver Junior Johnson, Wolfe might have dubbed him 'the last American hero'. Perhaps he also identified with this man who had devoted his life to 'pushing back the outside of the envelope'. In *The New Journalism* Wolfe describes (and demonstrates) the competitiveness between writers. He saw the same thing in flyers. The motivation was to be the best: 'A career in flying was like climbing one of those ancient Babylonian pyramids… the idea was to prove at every foot of the way up that pyramid that you were one of the elected and anointed ones who had *the right stuff*.'[11] And Yeager was the best, the flyer the astronauts looked up to. When you came right down to it, weren't the astronauts just lab rabbits in comparison, astro-chimps 'with a wire up the kazoo'?

## 3 Backstory: 1979–80

Although Tom Wolfe's reputation was enough to attract interest in Hollywood, *The Right Stuff* did not look like a sure-fire movie property. The book read like a novel, but the movie might look like a docu-drama. And then there was the structure. Wolfe begins with a character, Pete Conrad, who only becomes an astronaut *after* the Mercury programme is over. In fact, he begins with *Mrs* Pete Conrad. He then goes off on a tangent with Chuck Yeager, who broke the sound barrier ten years *before* Mercury got off the ground, and who played no part in the space programme. The only connection between Yeager and the astronauts was this abstract concept of Wolfe's own devising – 'the right stuff'. Even when we get to the recruitment of the astronauts, nearly ninety pages into the book, there are problems. For a start, there are seven of them. Wolfe scrupulously details each of the six flights (Slayton didn't fly because NASA discovered a minor cardiovascular condition), so even without Yeager this could be a long movie, a movie with six climaxes but no finale – no one gets to the moon in Wolfe's book, after all.

According to Steven Bach, then Head of Production at United Artists, the book was 'a dazzler', but it seemed to him two books:

One, a romantic elegy for a vanished code personified by … Yeager … the other was a razor-eyed chronicle of camaraderie, the Mercury astronauts… These two elements enriched the book but presented a danger for a movie because Yeager was so romantic, so appealing that one kept gravitating to him and away from the narrative, the obvious 'story' part that a movie could tell, which was the space programme … Besides, the triumph of the book wasn't the astronauts; it was the writing, that supersonic prose.[12]

For these reasons, Bach resisted overtures from independent producers Robert Chartoff and Irwin Winkler to acquire the property for them. Chartoff and Winkler (whose first property was a treatment by Tom Wolfe based on his Baby Jane Holzer story 'Girl of the Year'), had a track record of backing ambitious, risky projects – their most recent film had been *Raging Bull* (released in 1980). Since their surprise hit *Rocky*, they also had a good deal of clout to back up their exclusive deal at UA. Bach was outmanoeuvred, and UA paid half a million dollars for the rights.

As Bach describes it, Chartoff, Winkler and UA executives then discussed the perceived problem with the structure, and a suitable screenwriter to 'solve' it:

*Yeager wasn't a movie.* We threw him out again and concentrated on the astronauts, and that was worrisome, too, because we had a hunch that [UA President, Andreas] Albeck and the salespeople – with seven lead males to cast – were visualising Eastwood *and* Newman *and* Redford *and* Nicholson *and* Hoffman *and* McQueen *and*, for all we knew, Woody Allen for comic relief. We didn't encourage such fantasies, but neither did we stress the impossibility of making this a star movie. It was an ensemble piece, and the astronauts were too young to be played by established stars, all of whom had broken the forty barrier. This movie was about egomaniacally competitive jet jocks, who finally become, as Wolfe calls them, 'The Brotherhood', *buddies.* And just like that, the screenwriter's name tumbled into place.[13]

William Goldman was one of the best-known screenwriters in Hollywood. His credits included the Academy Award-winning *Butch Cassidy and the Sundance Kid*, a buddy movie which became one of the most successful Westerns ever made, as well as *All the President's Men, The Great Waldo Pepper* (about stunt flyers) and his novels *Marathon Man* and *Magic*. Goldman didn't come cheap, but for a prestigious project like this he was a natural candidate. Like Wolfe, he had a knack for the sucker punch, a hip, ironic sensibility camouflaging an underlying romanticism. In *Butch Cassidy and the Sundance Kid* he had rewritten history and made it seem fresh, virtually inventing the buddy picture in the process.

But Goldman agreed with his friend Bach. According to Goldman's *Adventures in the Screen Trade*, he couldn't reconcile the two thrusts of Wolfe's 'masterly' book:

I didn't know how to make it into a movie … And then Winkler totally turned me around. He … said that probably we should forget the Yeager material and go with the astronauts, starting with their selection, then their training, then the Alan Shepard flight, followed by the Gus Grissom fiasco, and climaxing the movie when John Glenn circled the Earth … Five acts.[14]

The desire to impose a linear, concerted dramatic structure on the material goes hand in glove with the Hollywood production system which, in 1980, was entering one of its most conservative phases. As Bach and Goldman imply, Hollywood's concept of what a movie is, or can be, is quite narrow: a story that can be broken down into 'acts'. Tom Wolfe wasn't a novelist. He hadn't written reportage at this length before, and somehow he had neglected to construct *The Right Stuff* in the appropriate manner (that is, in an *appropriable* manner). A screenwriter for hire, it was for Goldman to use his craftsmanship to reshape Wolfe's work, to chip away the rough edges to uncover the recognisable movie at its core. This is not to denigrate Goldman who, by his own account, connected with the material on an emotional and political level. Indeed, he says he became 'obsessed':

For the first time in my career, I wanted to write a movie that had a message. I wanted to 'say' something using *The Right Stuff* as a narrative vehicle. I wanted to 'say' something positive about America. Not patriotic in the John Wayne sense, but patriotic none the less – because the hostages had just been seized in Iran … the astronaut story paralleled the lack of confidence of the hostage crisis. The Russians were ahead. We were second rate. They put a dog in space. Our rockets exploded on the launching pad. Then, slowly, we began to get it together. When Alan Shepard was lobbed into the skies for fifteen minutes, small as that feat was compared to the Russian achievements, it *meant* something to the American people. And when John Glenn finally orbited four times around, we went crazy. We had, in our minds, caught up. We were America again.[15]

According to Steven Bach the patriotic fervour even reached UA's business affairs department, which handed over the biggest screenwriting cheque in the history of the company ($750,000). In May 1980, Goldman sent his first draft to Chartoff and Winkler, and in June, after adding at their behest what he describes as 'daredevil material' to the first act, the script was sent to UA. The studio gave the project the green light. Chartoff and Winkler were in the enviable position of having a 'go' project written by one of Hollywood's hottest screenwriters, based on a national bestseller, with a $20 million cheque in their pocket. Now they needed a director. Bach says that Goldman's *Butch Cassidy* collaborator George Roy Hill was the first choice, but he wanted to produce as well as direct. Goldman claims that 'everybody's first choice was Michael Ritchie (*Downhill Racer*, *The Candidate*) ... I thought him perfect; he is fast, prepared, good with men, and achieves a wonderful documentary look to his films.'[16] Then *The Island* came out, and Ritchie didn't look so perfect any more. *Rocky* director John Avildsen was next, but failed to agree terms. Only then did Philip Kaufman come on board.

Philip Kaufman was born in Chicago in 1936. He graduated from the University of Chicago in 1958, spent a year at Harvard Law School, and started an MA in American History at Chicago, which he did not complete ('instead I decided to become a mailman in California'). He had envisaged a career in teaching, but instead took off for Europe in the early 60s with his wife Rose. They lived in Greece, Israel, Holland and Italy. Inspired by Henry Miller, Kaufman tried to write a novel, then, returning to Chicago, he attempted to import the New Wave to America, writing and directing two quirky independent movies, *Goldstein* (1964) and *Fearless Frank* (1965, aka *Frank's Greatest Adventure*). Most modern reference books overlook these films completely, yet Jean Renoir said of *Goldstein* that it was the best American film he had seen in twenty years.[17] Based on Martin Buber's *Tales of the Hasidim*, it shared the Critics' Prize at Cannes in 1964 with Bertolucci's *Before the Revolution*. And *Fearless Frank*, released in 1969, marked the debut of a young actor called Jon Voight.

In 1967 Kaufman made his home in San Francisco, which serves as a useful symbol for his arm's-length relationship with Hollywood. (San Francisco is also a base for Kaufman's contemporaries, Francis Ford Coppola and George Lucas.) He signed a long-term contract with Universal, but it wasn't until 1971 that the studio belatedly allowed him to shoot his revisionist Western, *The Great Northfield Minnesota Raid*. Bewildered by Robert Duvall's portrait of Jesse James as a disturbed, sexually repressed psychopath, Universal sat on the film for a year, and then gave it only a token release. *The White Dawn* followed in 1974, for Paramount, with Warren Oates, Timothy Bottoms and Lou Gossett shipwrecked among the Eskimos. A hauntingly beautiful film based on anthropologist James Houston's novel, *The White Dawn* could scarcely have been less commercial, with a determinedly anti-heroic stance, an equally unromantic view of Eskimo life, and long passages devoid of either English dialogue or subtitles. Paramount had the film earmarked for Cannes, but then Coppola delivered *The Conversation* to them and they lost interest in Kaufman.

His bad luck continued. Scripts about Al Capone and Bob Dylan came to nought. He worked out a treatment with George Lucas, a tribute to 30s Saturday morning serials called *Raiders of the Lost Ark*, but the timing wasn't right. A project about Tom Horn by William Goldman ended in acrimony (though not between Kaufman and Goldman), and Kaufman fell out with his star Clint Eastwood a few weeks into shooting *The Outlaw Josey Wales* (1976). 'Clint often prints the first take,' Kaufman told *American Film* in 1983, proceeding to debunk another American hero. 'He's allergic to horses. So if I wanted a second take, especially on a horse, that created a problem.'[18]

After months preparing the first *Star Trek* movie in 1976, Paramount backed out at the last minute, informing Kaufman science fiction had no future – just weeks before *Star Wars* came out. Fortunately UA disagreed, and backed him to direct W. D. Richter's screenplay *Invasion of the Bodysnatchers* (1978), a sophisticated update of Don Siegel's 1956 classic. It was Kaufman's first commercial hit. Almost immediately he went on to make a long-nurtured adaptation of Richard Price's youth gang novel, *The Wanderers* (1979), which he had scripted with his wife Rose. Though it was overshadowed on release by Walter Hill's controversial *The Warriors*, like almost all Kaufman's films, it subsequently developed a cult audience.

Kaufman was the ideal candidate to direct *The Right Stuff*. He was the right age – twenty-five in 1961 – to remember the excitement of the space race. Indeed, his most recent film *The Wanderers* had been set in 1963, the year *The Right Stuff* ends.[19] A student of history, he has set most of his films in the past. A writer, he has gravitated towards literary adaptations (the exceptions being *Fearless Frank* and *The Great Northfield Minnesota Raid*).[20] He is interested in genre – in the Western, the youth drama, action-adventure and science fiction – but also in

subverting or redefining these traditional forms. In their concern for contemporary relevance – establishing a dialectic with the past – his films are very much of their time. His two Westerns – *Josey Wales* and *The Great Northfield Minnesota Raid* – share a mistrust of authority and an ambivalence towards their renegade 'heroes'. In *The White Dawn*, *The Wanderers* and, again, *Josey Wales*, he's fascinated with tribalism and makeshift communities, yet this must be set against the horror of the faceless universal conformity conceived of in *Invasion of the*

Clint Eastwood, who took over from Kaufman as director of *The Outlaw Josey Wales* (1976)

*Bodysnatchers*. (Like Howard Hawks before him, Kaufman values pluralism, but his individualistic communities are often at odds with their society. The integration of the outsider is not enough, if it is even possible.) The individual, in Kaufman's films, must be defined in an existential as well as a social sense. *The Great Northfield Minnesota Raid*, *The White Dawn*, and *Josey Wales* all share an interest in shamanism and mysticism, and Kaufman's interest in the cosmos is obvious in *Invasion of the Bodysnatchers* – in which the rational psychiatrist, played by Leonard Nimoy (Spock himself) is the friendly face of the enemy. As he told Stephen Farber in an interview in *Film Comment*:

*Bodysnatchers* deals, I think, with a sense of fear and a sense of awe: it's very healthy to unsettle people. Science fiction begins to give us a sense of mortality, a sense of things beyond us. It talks about things like deep space and cosmic consciousness. The humbling of humanity is important ... we need to be reminded that this is passing time.[21]

Kaufman's films don't simply express these values and concerns, they also embody them: in their extended casts and generous supply of intriguing character parts; their taste for travel and adventure; their vivid, earthy language and dynamic, resonant imagery; their narrative caprice and surprise; and their grounding in historical and ethnographic research (Clint Eastwood complained that Kaufman wanted to give *Josey Wales* a documentary feel). Like Wolfe, and to some extent like Goldman, there is an ironic, idiosyncratic tone, a sense of style which sometimes seems to betray the author's imaginative exhilaration in his subject's macho exploits. You might also draw a comparison between the liberating stylistic influence of the European New Wave, as Kaufman experienced it, and Tom Wolfe's rush to experiment with language in the New Journalism. Evidently, these are men of the same generation, if not quite the same politics. The title of Farber's *Film Comment* piece was 'Hollywood Maverick'. It concluded: 'So far, at least, Kaufman is a major artist in search of a major theme.'

On 21 July 1980, William Goldman and Philip Kaufman had their first script meeting. Goldman describes it in *Adventures in the Screen Trade*:

Within two minutes, I was into the nightmare.

I mentioned at the start how fortuitous the timing was, since there was going to be a rocket launch in Florida ... He said 'I'm not going to Florida, but there are some air shows up in Northern California I thought I'd catch.' Then I gave my pitch about the chance of making this patriotic movie and he said, 'I don't want to do that, patriotism's too easy, Ronald Reagan's patriotic and who wants that?' The entry I have in my journal for that day says: 'Kaufman meeting – disaster.' But in truth, I don't know which of his two remarks proved the most devastating. The one about patriotism

Left to right:
Chuck Yeager,
Sam Shepard and
Philip Kaufman

seems clearly the most potent. But the one about air shows meant old airplanes, and old airplanes meant one thing to me – Yeager.[22]

Kaufman recalls: 'I looked at the script – and I like [Goldman's] writing and so forth – but I said, "That's all well and good, but you've left out the right stuff. It's called *The Right Stuff* but the right stuff isn't there. This is not a story of the astronauts, it's the story of the test pilots, the story of Chuck Yeager".'

For Kaufman, Yeager was the heart and soul of Tom Wolfe's book. In setting out to explore the near-kamikaze courage of the astronauts, Wolfe had found instead the test pilots' fraternal code, which he relates to the Calvinist notion of predestination: 'The idea was to prove ... you were one of the elected and annointed ones who had *the right stuff*.' It transcends courage:

As to what this ineffable quality was ... well, it obviously involved bravery. But it was not bravery in the simple sense of being willing to risk your life. The idea seemed to be that any fool could do that ... the idea here ... seemed to be that a man should have the ability to go up in a hurtling piece of machinery and put his hide on the line and then have the moxie, the reflexes, the experience, the coolness, to pull it back in the last yawning moment – and then go up again *the next day*, and the next day, and every next day, even if the series should prove infinite – and ultimately, in its best expression, do so in a cause that means something to thousands, to a people, a nation, to humanity, to God.[23]

Yeager had it, clearly. But did the Mercury astronauts? They risked their lives, but what of the moxie, the coolness? Levered into their fully automated space capsules, they weren't pilots, they were 'spam in the can'. Wolfe gives the realisation to Glenn in what was seen as his moment of triumph, plunging back into the earth's atmosphere with a faulty heat shield:

If the heat shield came off, then he would fry. If they didn't want him – *the pilot!* – to know all this, then it meant they were afraid he might panic. And if he didn't even *need* to know the whole pattern – just the pieces, so he could follow orders – *then he wasn't really a pilot!* ... He was being treated like a passenger – a redundant component, a backup engineer, a boiler-room attendant – in an automatic system! – like someone who did not have that rare and unutterably righteous stuff! – as if the right stuff itself did not even matter! It was a transgression against all that was holy.

Even though the astronauts don't measure up to the test pilots' strict understanding of the right stuff – and Wolfe goes back to Yeager in his NF-104 at the end of the book to underline the point – they reach the top of the pyramid nevertheless. The world has changed, and in this new brave world the astronauts are the annointed ones. 'Cold Warriors of the Heavens', Wolfe calls them. Glenn survives his descent:

He could hear the Cape capcom:
'How are you doing?'
'Oh, pretty good.'
*Oh, pretty good.* It wasn't Yeager, but it wasn't bad.

Kaufman wrote thirty-five pages of notes which he sent to Goldman and the producers. According to Steven Bach, who is sympathetic to Goldman, this memo 'virtually rewrote the screenplay'. Goldman quotes its opening: 'This is a Search film, a quest for a certain quality that has seen its best days ...' The memo ended with a list of 'Search' movies: *The Searchers*, *La Dolce Vita*, *La Grande Illusion* and others (Goldman doesn't specify). 'Many of them have a rambling form, but a compelling theme,' concluded Kaufman. 'They are episodic, "Truth" is found along the way. And in all of them, it seems, we detect the passing of a higher quality.'[24]

The debate wasn't just about different interpretations of 'the right stuff', it was explicitly political. Bach: 'Bill [Goldman] was passionate to say something about the right stuff *now*, not *then*, and deeply feared that Phil's phrase *the passing of a higher quality* was the antithesis of everything he wanted to do.'[25] 'I wanted to say ... that America was still a great place,' Goldman explains. 'What Phil wanted to say was that America was going down the tubes. That it *had* been great once, but those days were gone, and wasn't that a shame.'[26]

Just as the Mercury programme was dictated by Cold War paranoia, and, later, John Kennedy was determined to put a man on the moon as a national morale booster (the ultimate imperialism, the stars and stripes on the moon, no expense spared),[27] so in the summer of 1980, with Ronald Reagan heading for the White House, the argument over the conception of the film of *The Right Stuff* was dominated by questions of patriotism. In 1962 John Glenn unconsciously tapped into white America's sense of its own destiny, reviving the heroic myth of the pioneer spirit. That's what Goldman wanted to get at. After the Soviet invasion of Afghanistan, the Cold War was back on. America was to boycott the Moscow Olympics, and Reagan would soon be talking about the 'Evil Empire'. But the legacy of Jimmy Carter's administration – blighted by the prolonged hostage crisis in Iran – seemed to be despair. Goldman wanted to revive America's pride. Kaufman claims the impasse reached the point where Goldman wrote a letter to the studio and the producers calling him 'fundamentally anti-American'.[28]

One can only speculate what a Goldman-Avildsen version of *The Right Stuff* might have looked like – *Top Gun in Space,* perhaps – though John Glenn, (now Democratic Senator John Glenn) on seeing the script called it 'Laurel and Hardy Go to Space'. Perhaps surprisingly, faced with a straight choice between their screenwriter and their director, Chartoff and Winkler stood by the latter. In *Adventures in the Screen Trade*, the moral of Goldman's story comes down to the position of the screenwriter: 'I may have never felt, in movies, such impotence as during *The Right Stuff* meetings. Whenever someone asks "How much power does a screenwriter have?" my mind now goes only to those terrible days … The answer, now and forever: in the crunch, none.'[29]

According to Kaufman, Goldman 'neglected to mention that he only had a two-week window to do the rewrite before he went on to another project, so he didn't want to tamper too much with what he had'. Furthermore, Winkler disputes Goldman's recollection that he, Winkler, argued against Kaufman and Chartoff on the screenwriter's behalf.[30]

Goldman quit the film, and Kaufman proceeded to write his own screenplay in eight weeks,

## 4 *The Right Stuff*

As the Ladd Company logo gives way to a black screen, we hear the
sound of the upper atmosphere, a distant howling void. A new note, a
percussive echo chamber, builds into a curt, abrasive tattoo which cues
the blast of a synthesised fanfare – the principal motif in this score –
which trumpets the main title, white on black: *The Right Stuff*. Behind
the fanfare, the atmospheric noise soars. It might be a jet plane
whooshing through the air but, again, it's synthesised, abstracted. It is
difficult to be certain what is an effect and what comes from composer
Bill Conti.[31] Kaufman had experimented with sound before, most
notably on *Invasion of the Bodysnatchers*. Here he could go much further.
He had twenty-eight sound-effects experts working on the film, and
would overhaul the soundtrack three times before he was through.

The first image we see appears to be taken from the nose of a
plane as it cuts through the clouds and then banks off to the right.[32]
It is in black and white, and could be in slow motion, but the surging
forward momentum picks up with the thrust of the music. We dissolve
to similar, increasingly rapid shots as the voice-over begins: 'There was a
demon that lived in the air. They said whoever challenged him would
die. Their controls would freeze up, their planes would buffet wildly, and
they would disintegrate …' The voice is male, folksy, with a backwoods
flavour. It belongs to Levon Helm of The Band, who plays Yeager's
engineer, Ridley.[33] 'The demon lived at Mach 1 on the meter: 750 miles
an hour, where the air can no longer move out of the way. He lived
behind a barrier through which they said *no* man could ever pass. They
called it, "the sound barrier".'

As Helm pronounces 'the sound barrier', there is an ominous,
percussive death rattle on the soundtrack. A subtle cut: from the clouds
to smoke snaking around a 1940s plane as it refuels on the ground. Men
stand in front of the plane. We're still in monochrome, and there is a
scratch running down the middle of the frame. But this isn't
documentary footage, it has been artificially degraded by maximising

contrast and adding dirt to the print; the smoke suggests a mythical quality – like the steam which swirls about the cab in the opening of *Taxi Driver* – and the men are actors. We cut closer. They are all in fighter jackets, chewing gum. One of them is Sam Shepard – Yeager. The voice-over continues: 'Then they built a small plane, the X-1, to break the sound barrier. And men came to the high desert of California to ride it. They were called "test pilots", and no one knew their names.'

That's it from the voice-over, for the next three hours and five minutes, at any rate. Kaufman is too good a film-maker to need a prompter – if you can show, why tell? – but the use of the voice-over supplies tricky technical information succinctly and sets the tone – colloquial, almost fairytale. Despite the 'documentary' visuals, the sound barrier is 'a demon'; already we know we're in for more than a science project. The voice-over stresses the anonymity of the pilots, establishing perhaps the biggest single distinction between Yeager's experience in 1947 and that of the astronauts a decade later.

Next we see footage of a propeller plane, a B-29, taking off, carrying the X-1 test plane beneath it. In the first shot in this sequence, the moon – the project's ultimate destination – is visible behind the wing of the plane. Here, however, any mythical element is serendipitous: this is genuine archive footage from the 40s. Before shooting even began, researchers trawled through film libraries to collate aviation footage, newsreel material, footage of rocket launches. They eventually work-printed more than 300,000 feet of it (for comparison, *The Right Stuff* itself runs to 17,334 feet) either for inclusion in the film or simply for reference.

With the end of the voice track, Kaufman drops in isolated sound effects: the propellers, some crackle on the intercom. The music swells into Conti's main theme. The X-1 is released from the B-29, and archive footage is mixed with point-of-view shots, from the X-1, surging through the clouds. The pilot's voice counts off from the Machmeter – 9.2, 9.3, 9.4 – becoming higher pitched and more distorted as he approaches the magical Mach 1. The camera tries to follow the X-1, but jerkily, the plane is too fast. The cutting becomes faster too. Back to the point-of-view shots. The camera/plane twists on its axis and appears to spin out of control. The count ends in an explosion at 9.9: not the supersonic boom, but the test plane crashing to the ground. The film bursts into colour with the orange, yellow and red flames of the explosion, and the picture ratio switches from the square 1: 1.33 to the 'scope 1: 2.33 frame. The audacity of the cut (reminiscent of the first cut in Welles's *Touch of Evil*) heightens the impact of the explosion and marks the end of the preamble. This dramatic crash is the movie's take-off point. The sudden shift to colour and widescreen heightens our appreciation of these aesthetic pleasures. It's a bold announcement of the scale of this picture.

Kaufman doesn't dwell on the flames, but instead pulls off another shock-cut, to a woman waking bolt upright, as if from a nightmare. We

Faked archive footage filmed at Edwards Airforce Base

deduce that her nightmare has already come true: her husband is dead. A man in black – Royal Dano (listed in the credits simply as 'Minister') – walks slowly up the pathway to her home. The woman has tears in her eyes, a child in her arms. As he approaches, Dano removes his black hat. (Wolfe began with the wives too, with the nightmare that some 'solemn friend of Widows and Orphans' would come home instead of your husband . . .) Now he is leading the hymn 'for those in peril in the air' at the funeral service, on some desert hilltop above the air base, Joshua trees and mourners in silhouette against the twilight. The tall, gaunt Dano serves as a symbol of death in the film. He will sup beer quietly in the corner of Pancho's bar, and will be on hand down at Cape Canaveral for Alan Shepard's brush with mortality. He always wears his black preacher's garb but it looks anachronistic even for the period. He brings no sense of religion to the film beyond the ritualistic – hymns apart, he has no lines. Dano, who had a colourful bit part in *The Great Northfield Minnesota Raid*, brings with him the resonances of a long career as a character actor in Hollywood, stretching back to his role as The Tattered Man in *The Red Badge of Courage* (John Huston, 1951), and a couple of Westerns apiece with Nick Ray and Anthony Mann. This funeral service seems to belong in one of those older films: the self-consciously

Under Western skies …

'Romantic' compositional sense, the rhetorical crane shot at the end, and the 'Technicolor' sunset evoke John Ford and George Stevens, even *Gone With the Wind*.

Also in attendance, bar-owner Pancho Barnes (Kim Stanley), Glennis Yeager (Barbara Hershey), pilot Slick Goodlin (William Russ), Ridley and Chuck Yeager. Yeager stands apart from the rest. Cinematographer Caleb Deschanel has photographed him alone, with the full benefit of the setting sun. He's almost glowing. A swift exchange of glances is the only hint that the Yeagers might be a couple. In contrast to Ridley, who is in full dress uniform, Yeager wears his soft leather flying jacket, with the collar turned up. Coming in for a close-up as three planes fly by overhead, Deschanel shoots him from a low, heroic angle. He is chewing gum, apparently more interested in the planes than the dead man (the attitude is straight from Howard Hawks's *Only Angels Have Wings*).

Kaufman's screenplay describes the next sequence:

*Exterior. The High Desert. Day.*
*A Rider* on horseback moves across the gnarled and twisted panorama of Joshua trees which stand out in silhouette on the fossil wasteland like some arthritic nightmare.
*Close Up. Yeager.* He's wearing a leather jacket. WWII pilot style, and the look is more John Garfield than John Wayne. Wind blows tumbleweed along the trail.
*He sees*: a lonely airbase: two Quonset-style hangars, a couple of gasoline pumps, a single concrete runway, a few tarpaper shacks, and some tents ... There's something about the flapping tents, the howling wind ... And the Small Evil Little Plane (the X-1 rocket: 'looked like a fat orange swallow with white markings, but really just a length of pipe with four rocket chambers in it') that gives the feeling Something is about to happen here. And there's something in the way Yeager looks at the plane ... and the plane seems almost to look at him (like the bronc that can't be broken) ... that tells us these two souls will meet again. The X-1's rockets are screaming. The sound growing louder, more ominous ... louder and louder.

This is exceptionally evocative screenwriting – the sort screenwriters are taught to shy away from lest they intimidate the director. Perhaps only a writer-director could have written it. There is no comparable scene in Wolfe, but the passage is steeped in Wolfe's rhythms: the repetitions and especially that Small Evil Little Plane. And it works better on camera. Kaufman told *Cahiers du Cinéma* that the film 'was made in answer to the question, what happened to the Western?' In this sequence, you might say that the Western – a lone man on horseback – confronts science fiction. The cowboy stares at a technological future he can barely imagine (but we know), and asks himself, can he ride it? It's an indelible image, one of Kaufman's most resonant, recalling Cole Younger's wonderment at a traction engine in *The Great Northfield Minnesota Raid*. After the economy of the preceding sequences, he allows Shepard/Yeager nearly two minutes just psyching out the plane, cutting from the Rider's intent stare to the plane and back, like gunslingers waiting for the draw. Conti bolsters the image with an echoing dramatic chord, a metallic shunt which gives the machine a voice. In fact, the staging is simpler than in the screenplay: there are no hangars, just a stretch of empty desert. The isolation heightens the strange dramatic force of the moment. The flames licking from the rear of the X-1, and the heat haze they give off . . . it's George and the dragon, the demon that lives in the sky.

Sam Shepard doesn't act in this film. He doesn't have to. The performance is a taciturn squint and a stick of gum, but the look speaks volumes. Kaufman recalled: 'Anthony Mann once told me, "Gary Cooper on a horse *is* a scene". I felt Sam was a scene.'[34] Though he cast the astronauts with an eye on their real-life counterparts, the rangy, slender Shepard looks nothing like Chuck Yeager, 'a short, wiry but muscular little guy with dark curly hair'.[35] Then again, Yeager didn't have a public face. If there was a star role in the movie it was Yeager. But Eastwood had made Kaufman wary of stars: 'Stars get chickenshit… they're so afraid to lose their star status. There should be an "acteur" theory of film-making. They want to shape an entire movie around their persona.'[36]

Shepard wasn't a star, but he was an icon – 'the icon of the id', according to *Time*. He had appeared in a handful of films – *Days of Heaven*, *Raggedy Man*, *Frances* – but had defined himself predominantly outside showbusiness circles, 'off-off' Broadway (such was his diffidence towards stardom that he insisted on a no-press clause in his contract). His plays – *True West*, *Fool for Love*, *Buried Child* – are infected with the mythology of Hollywood and the West, but not in thrall to it. The infection is part of what they are about. Like Yeager, Shepard stands apart. Deschanel shoots him in a soft, romantic light which brings out the 'bruised, mysterious ... shyness' Kaufman saw in him, along with his 'sense of danger'.[37] He cast him for 'his intense dedication to the manly life, rejecting New York, the taste for cowboys and rodeos – and all with the look of a man in a leather jacket on a horse meeting a jet plane in the desert'.[38]

In another regard, however, Shepard was fundamentally ill-equipped to play Yeager. Like Travis in *Paris, Texas*, he refuses to fly. 'I admit to an overwhelming vertigo that I don't quite understand and I'm unwilling to psychoanalyse. Suffice it to say, it's a severe problem of the imagination. The inability to control mental picturings of stupefying heights ... the absolutely realistic sensation of falling without end, for

Kim Stanley as Pancho Barnes

instance. That's one I have no power over.'[39] This particular irony, the film-makers did their best to suppress.

Pancho's Fly Inn was the watering hole at Muroc Field. 'Nobody putting together such a place for a movie about flying in the old days would ever dare make it as dilapidated and generally go-to-hell as it actually was,' writes Wolfe (in real life, as in the film, it burnt down). With its corral and swing doors, Pancho's reminds us again of the Western. Yeager enters and stands just inside, artfully backlit, 'like some lame goddamn mouseshit sheepherder', in Pancho's words. The phrase comes from Wolfe. Throughout the film, Kaufman picks up on words and phrases from the book and puts them into the mouths of the characters – a technique he would use again when adapting Milan Kundera's *The Unbearable Lightness of Being*. 'You almost have to get

The hall of fame at Pancho's Fly Inn

inside the author's words and let them become a mantra to you,' Kaufman says. 'Follow that mantra. Let it speak to you as you're writing.'

The real Pancho Barnes deserves a film of her own. A California socialite, she ran guns for the Mexican revolutionaries, broke the air-speed record for women in 1930, and became the star attraction in 'Pancho Barnes's Mystery Circus of the Air' before settling at Muroc. It is Pancho who puts a name to 'the Rider': 'Yeager'. Even more than Glennis Yeager, Pancho is an honorary member of 'the brethren'. When Yeager enters the bar we see her putting a picture up on the wall of a pilot who has been killed. This business of commemorating the dead aviators is pure Kaufman. It is a graphic representation of the mortality rate at Muroc, and also establishes Pancho's as both the literal and metaphorical clubhouse of the right stuff. When he arrives at Edwards, as Muroc was later renamed, Gordo Cooper will signal his immaturity and 'pudknocker' status by boasting that his picture will soon be on the wall.

Yeager and Pancho exchange talismans. He gives her a snake's rattle, she gives him his bottle of whisky. He goes over to join Ridley and begins fiddling with a football helmet Ridley has found for him (crash helmets for pilots have not yet been devised). But the focus of the scene shifts: men in suits, in company with military officers, are negotiating with Slick. They want him to break the sound barrier but, he reiterates, 'Some people say the sound barrier can't be broke ... the sound barrier's a farm you can buy in the sky.' He wants $150,000. Too much. The liaison man (David Clennon) redirects their attention to Yeager. Clennon's role is choric: now he fills in Yeager's military record. Later he will watch, bemused, as the astronauts are greeted like heroes at their first press conference, and comment disparagingly on Gus Grissom's flight. Though no such character appears in the book, most of his dialogue comes straight from Wolfe. Tellingly – it signals his remove from society – Yeager takes the job for nothing ('The Air Force is paying me already, ain't that right, sir?'), though Pancho offers her own incentive: a free steak (again, it smacks of *Only Angels Have Wings*).

Glennis enters during this exchange. One of the suits mistakenly assumes she's a waitress, but she knocks back a drink at the bar. Like Pancho, she wears trousers, and carries herself with self-assurance. But Glennis is not masculinised. 'Glamorous Glennis', Yeager dubs the X-1. He flirts with her ('You ever been caught out in the desert alone?') but she gives as good as she gets ('Never did meet the man who could catch me out there'. 'I'm half jackrabbit,' he rejoins). The sexual banter is yet another throwback to classic Hollywood – Hawks, particularly. It could be argued that, like Fassbinder in *Veronika Voss* or *Lili Marleen*, Kaufman is recreating the period by drawing on our familiarity with the films of the time, using 'style' as a period signifier – a more sophisticated version of the use of faked documentary material. But it's also a way of

Frenchy's, in Howard Hawks' *Only Angels Have Wings*

contextualising the events not in a specific timeframe, but in the nobler realm of Hollywood legend. You sense that Yeager is not a man but an archetype, the personification of the heroic ideal as the movies taught it in the 40s. Either way, Yeager is bound to the past. If the real Yeager was motivated by simple militarism and would 'surprise' Kaufman by cashing in on his belated fame in numerous advertisements (endorsing everything from aviator sunglasses to whisky), the director's mythic

Yeager is untainted by contemporary capitalist concerns for fame or money.

The flirtation is a put-on: Glennis and Chuck are married.[40] We see them racing breathlessly through the desert on horseback, their panting hot and heavy – it's as close to sex as the movie gets. Good as her word, Glennis is faster than her husband, and the sequence reveals a marriage of equals – another contrast with the astronauts. But the prime reason for the scene is to get Yeager thrown from his horse and left rolling on the ground, clutching his side.

It is a fact that Chuck Yeager broke the sound barrier on 14 October 1947 with a couple of broken ribs – and that his flight engineer, Ridley, enabled the injured pilot to snap shut the cockpit door by sawing off about nine inches from a broom handle, a discreet late addition to

The X-1, steaming

the supersonic technology the Air Force had provided. Tom Wolfe seized with glee on these details – braver, funnier and far more human than fiction – and look how Kaufman extrapolates them into cinema: Yeager's painful embrace from Pancho beside the steaming jet plane; Glennis swiftly helping him into his jacket before anyone can notice his discomfort; Ridley's no-nonsense ingenuity (the janitor is using the broom at the time) and the triumphant twirl he gives the sawn-off handle, like a cheerleader's baton … and then the director's sweetest comic inspiration, the janitor left stranded with his back-breaking, decapitated broom.

The flight itself is a *tour de force*. We're twenty minutes into the film and this is what we've been waiting for, the showdown between man, machine and the elements. A date caption underlines the sense of occasion. Bill Conti gets his first chance to stretch – with a nod to Tchaikovsky's violin concerto – as Kaufman establishes the triangle of interest: military officials, Pancho, Glennis and Royal Dano waiting anxiously on the ground; Ridley in the B-29; and Yeager mounting the X-1:

RIDLEY: There she is, partner, all bridled and saddled and ready to go.
YEAGER: Ridley, you got any Beemans [gum]? Loan me some will ya? I'll pay you back later.

(Top) Pushing the outside of the envelope
(Bottom) Breaking the sound barrier

The ground shots were filmed on location on the very airstrip that Yeager used, and some of the occasional B-29 exteriors are genuine, but the X-1 presented the film-makers with more of a challenge. Though they were able to hire jets from the West German Air Force to stand in for the NF-104 for part of Yeager's climactic flight, most of the aerospace shots feature models. Kaufman was adamant that state-of-the-art motion control and blue-screen effects were not appropriate for this film:

*The Right Stuff* was more of a jerryrigged movie ... I wanted the effects to capture that ratshack quality, like when Yeager used a broom handle to close the door of his X-1. The planes were always on the verge of falling apart, and we needed to capture that danger. We spent about a year trying to do them the way ILM [George Lucas's company, responsible for *Star Wars*] would do them, with everything that was available at the time, but I found that that look might work for spaceships over alien planets, but airships over this earth just don't work that way. Real planes have a sense of weight. So after almost a year I just threw all that stuff out ... I thought surely we can go back to a simpler way of doing this.

The special-effects team studied old films, including *The Sound Barrier* and *Flying Tigers* to get a sense of what Kaufman was after. They watched Howard Hughes's *Jet Pilot* (shot by Josef von Sternberg in 1950, but unreleased for seven years) with particular interest: it was the last time the X-1 flew ... one Chuck Yeager had been at the controls. They aimed for a jerky camera style, recreating the 'slippage' of the plane within the frame. In other words, contrary to the 'invisible camera' Hollywood conventionally deems necessary for the suspension of disbelief, this film works on our understanding of the limitations of the camera – actually exaggerating those limitations – to create its illusion of reality.

Three scaled models of the X-1 and the X-1A, ranging from 18 to 122 centimetres in length, were built in fibreglass and foam. Cameraman

John Fante conducted experiments with an Eyemo, a small football-shaped 35mm camera which had been used as gunsight point camera in World War Two, and which is now used principally as a crash camera. He would run towards the models suspended on bungy cords, or even ride past them in a wheelchair. For other shots, to create the camera jiggle, the team attached a variable-speed massager to a telephoto lens (the telephoto was deemed more 'realistic' than wide-angle, because that's what Air Force chaser planes would have used).

Eventually, varying the frame rates from between twelve to 110 frames per second, they found their way right back to basics, throwing models from a third-floor window, with a large-scale canvas painting of the desert below, or shooting them up into the sky from a crossbow. They attached them to weights and helium balloons, and sent them careering down eighty-foot wires suspended from a man-lift. In the end, only John Glenn's orbit utilised conventional motion-control blue-screen work.[41]

When the X-1 drops from the B-29, and Yeager flicks the switch, it takes off like – a rocket! The cutting in the film is generally very rapid (there are 2,750 cuts in total, about five times the average for a two-hour feature), but there are more than 130 cuts in this four-minute flight sequence alone. The choppiness doesn't simply impart a sense of speed, it emphasises the buffeting the plane is taking. Inside the cockpit, everything is ashudder. The X-1 flies from right to left, and left to right. Sometimes it seems to be arcing up, sometimes it's horizontal. If we're disorientated, that's part of the ride.

How to show the breaking of the sound barrier presented its own problems – by its very nature, it defies recording (a sonic boom is caused by the tear in the pocket of airwaves which accumulates at the front of a plane flying at Mach 1; the boom might be described as sound turned inside out). In the film, the boom is a mix of explosions, predominantly primer cord, which incinerates at 23,000 feet per second. This first explosion became the basis for all the subsequent rocket blast-offs, which build up throughout the film, each incorporating the cumulative

(Overleaf) On a wing and a prayer

boom and adding to it (there's even said to be a pig scream in there somewhere).

Once Yeager has gone through the barrier, Clennon the liaison officer runs to the phone to break the good news, but he's restrained by a major who explains that press coverage is forbidden for reasons of national security. It is the beginning of the Cold War. Yeager's triumph is self-sufficient in any case. There he is, standing tall on the wing of the tamed X-1, saluting the sky. 'Word will get out,' Clennon tells the major that night. 'Pretty soon every fighter jock, every rocket ace, every rat racer in the country will be headed this way. Each one of them wanting to push the outside of the envelope and get to the top of the pyramid.' Again, his words come from Wolfe – this is the very rationale on which *The Right Stuff* is built. The standard has been set, now it will be put to the test. Outside, the Yeagers drink and laugh and howl at the full moon, and there's a country and western tune on the juke-box, something about the lure of faraway places, 'calling . . . calling me'.

Kaufman cuts from the moon to an open-top car driving through the desert in the full brightness of the day. Even before we've read the caption, we know we're in the 50s from the rock 'n' roll song on the car radio: 'I've got a rocket in my pocket . . .'. Six years have passed, but here is Gordo Cooper (Dennis Quaid) arriving at Edwards in fulfilment of Clennon's prophecy. Gordo even echoes Clennon's – that is, Wolfe's – pyramid metaphor. With him are his wife Trudy (Pamela Reed) and their two daughters. 'This is the place to be . . . Just a matter of time before we get ourselves worked our way up that old ladder,' Gordo tells Trudy.

Structurally this is an important scene, twenty-five minutes into the film, moving us on in time and switching the perspective to the first of the astronauts. The biggest problem was always linking the Yeager story with the astronauts, but Kaufman finds the overlap he needs at Edwards air base: he presents Cooper, Deke Slayton (Scott Paulin) and Gus Grissom (Fred Ward) as admiring acolytes of Yeager's right stuff. In doing so he dramatises the pyramidal class system Wolfe describes and gives Yeager a personal investment in the astronauts' lives – he's there when the government comes to recruit test pilots for Mercury, and he's listening in on the radio during their first press conference. All this is historically justifiable, with three provisos: Grissom was never at Edwards (though he had known Gordo Cooper before), NASA never sent scouts there for astronauts, and Yeager was based elsewhere between 1954 and 1961.

Even with this sleight of hand, the structure of the film remains highly unconventional, switching between five identification figures – Yeager and four of the astronauts[42] – over a sixteen-year period. Much of the film's symmetry and sense of cohesion derive not from narrative action but from the cyclical repetition of several key lines, their import shifting subtly each time, taking on levels of irony and even wisdom, and becoming, in Kaufman's phrase, mantra-like. 'Pushing the outside of the envelope' is one such line. 'No bucks, no Buck Rogers,' is another, which Gus Grissom will turn around and throw back in the faces of the NASA scientists. Even more important is the exchange between the Coopers, when Gordo asks Trudy, 'Who's the best pilot you ever saw?', just as he will (with far less conviction) when, en route to the Lovelace Clinic, he asks her to play the happy housewife for the benefit of public relations. At the end, the question will be turned back on him, and his answer will mark both his own maturity and the reconciliation of Yeager, the astronauts, and the right stuff.

For now, this first scene with Cooper sets up a number of contrasts. First the music, which signals the new mood of the new decade. Then Gordo and Chuck: he's here to emulate Yeager and surpass him ('Who's the best pilot you ever saw? You're looking at him, baby'). Gordo is boastful, human; Yeager laconic, heroic. Also the Yeagers and the Coopers: the former sexual, equal, independent, living in the present; the latter parental (Trudy is as concerned with the girls as with Gordo), unequal ('We?' Trudy challenges him, 'You mean, "you"'), dependent, living for the future ('I move up, you move up, right to the top of the old pyramid'). The location – a convertible – suggests both movement and transience. Trudy will soon complain to the other flyers' wives that her old friends are full of the 'cutthroat world' of their husbands' Madison Avenue jobs (as if *they* faced a twenty-three per cent death rate). But the contrast is also a comparison: the Coopers are the optimistic face of the American Dream as it was understood in the 50s, looking to get ahead as if it is their birthright. Dennis Quaid plays Gordo with a charismatic swagger and a wide, 100-watt grin, but he's balanced by Trudy's caginess. They're shot apart, in individual close-ups, only coming together for the final two-shot ('Hey, have I ever let you down?'). Even here, Trudy pointedly looks off into the distance.

The next cut wittily undermines Gordo's cockiness: brown sludge trickles out of a basin tap – which comes off in Trudy's hand. It's also a

Pamela Reed as Trudy Cooper

sexual image. Gordo makes the most noise about his machismo, and Kaufman extracts a number of laughs at his expense. There is no doubt that Trudy is the more sensitive, sensible and mature of the two. Gordo is all mouth, and she's all eyes. There is a poignant moment when, setting up house in the unwelcoming air base, Trudy is jolted by the distant explosion of a plane crash. She runs to check on Gordo, and is relieved to find him snoring on the sofa ... but then her gaze turns outside, to the two girls playing with a toy plane in the garden, and beyond – a very rare zoom shot from Deschanel – to the black smoke on the horizon.

The strain on the wives is keenly expressed. As Gordo renews his acquaintance with Gus and makes his *faux pas* over the photographs on Pancho's wall, the Slaytons are arguing in the background about what is

Drinking to success

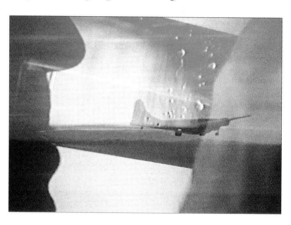

evidently the latest in a long list of fatal accidents. Later, while Deke, Gus and Gordo barbecue outside, with their thoughts on Yeager, the wives – Marge (Mickey Crocker), Betty (Veronica Cartwright) and Trudy – share their fears and frustrations. 'Men are such assholes,' they conclude, then laugh at their own temerity. Trudy, it emerges, has decided to leave Gordo. Outside, meanwhile, the men have let the barbecue get out of control. Gordo skewers a flaming sausage and shouts to his wife, would she like a hot dog ...? Not just a phallic gag, since we have already learned that Gordo's nickname is 'Hot Dog'. The shot, with Trudy looking out from the house into the garden, is a clear echo of the scene in which she saw the crash. As she backs off in horror, the camera pans to the window, where we see the reflection of that same horizon.

The style of these scenes is markedly different from what has gone before, even though many of the same locations and characters (Pancho, the Yeagers, Clennon, the Minister) appear. The romantic aura of the sound barrier passage, signalled by the 'magic hour' light – dawn for the X-1 flight, sunset before it – the evocations of the Western in the desert landscapes and artful framing ... these have given way in the 50s to a harder, midday light. Trudy might be one of Edward Hopper's lonely

Kaufman directs
Harry Shearer (left)
and Jeff Goldblum
(right)

models, sitting on the bed, hugging a pillow to her chest, framed by the doorway. The desert has been domesticated (barbecues on the lawn, white picket fences), and even Pancho's has lost some of its old charm: it's crowded now, and there are no horses in the corral. Civilisation has come to the wilderness: America's triumph, according to John Ford, and its tragedy.

When we see Scott Crossfield's record-breaking Mach 2 airspeed on black-and-white newsreel, it's clear how much has changed. It's a field day for the press. They're everywhere, pushing to get a better view as Yeager (unnamed by the newsreel commentary) congratulates his rival. The press plays a significant role in the film. Tom Wolfe describes them as 'the Animal', 'squatting and crawling … their cameras screwed into their eye sockets, like a swarm of root weevils'. Kaufman takes the image and runs with it: the press photographers are played by members of I Fratelli Bologna, a group of acrobats, jugglers, mime artists and clowns. Their every appearance is heralded by a low scraping, scavenging insect sound made up of flashbulbs popping, a locust swarm, and three women chewing carrots.[43] The paparazzi are like a parasitic plague, the boldest indication yet of the direction the film will take.

'Those root weevils write history,' Clennon tells Yeager in Pancho's bar. 'You know what really makes your rocket ships go up? Funding, that's what. No bucks, no Buck Rogers.' Yeager is idly running a dime over his knuckles. Across the room, Gordo mimics him. Crossfield celebrates his record with a complimentary steak, and Glennis says hello to Fred, the barman (played by Chuck Yeager, who served as a technical consultant on the film). Kaufman indulges the Yeagers with a slow waltz and then dissolves from a close-up of the whisky Chuck drinks down to his dawn take-off in the X-1A: amber is the colour of Yeager's quiet courage.

'December 12, 1953', the caption says. Yeager climbs into the cockpit. 'Hey Ridley, you got any Beemans? Well, loan me some will ya, I'll pay you back later.' This time he has a crash helmet worthy of the name – with a visor! – and the sequence is simpler, shorter than his flight in '47, but shot in the same way, with cutaways to the ground where Cooper, Grissom and Slayton listen in on the shortwave. Simpler, that is, until he's gone through Mach 2 and beaten Crossfield's record. Ridley tells him to ease off, but Yeager's hunting down the demon. At Mach 2.5 a synth chord sounds a distant echo of *2001*, and Yeager (his visor mirroring Keir Dullea/Dave's in Kubrick's film) approaches his own mysterious stargate … a kaleidoscopic whirlpool, deep, deep blue revolving about a central black hole. He blacks out and the plane goes

into freefall. But Yeager has the right stuff, and he pulls out in time.
'We sure chased that old demon that time ... What's next, Ridley?'

What's next is a dissolve to a rocket launch pad, captioned 'Star City,
Russia. October 4, 1957', and scored to a mordant balalaika.[44] Ridley
has pronounced Mach 2.5 'fast as a man could go', setting the seal on
Yeager's triumph. The only way is up. The lift-off is successful (we see
Wolfe's shadowy 'Grand Designer', Edward Anhalt, laughing in triumph
through the afterburn). The space race is on, and the Soviets are in
front.

Another caption: 'Washington, DC'. The camera is at ground level,
chasing a man in a suit – Jeff Goldblum – as he runs down a long

Nurse Murch
puts the pilots'
machismo to the
test at the Lovelace
Clinic

corridor. This shot will be repeated, as will the Star City montage, as the
Soviets succeed in putting a man in space; a running gag indeed. The
montage is a nightmare of Soviet superiority, a projection of the 'red
menace' literal enough to apply a red filter. The Washington shot is also
quite literal: panic in the corridors of power. This is shorthand, but also
comic exaggeration. At the end of the corridor is a darkened conference
room. Here the President has convened a war counsel. Wolfe allowed

himself a wry smile at the Cold War paranoia of the times, but Kaufman goes for all-out satire, ridiculing the government as incompetent buffoons, incapable even of working a projector. Lyndon Johnson bears the brunt of this, Donald Moffat (a Kaufman regular) caricaturing him – unfairly – as a pompous, Commie-bashing publicity hound. Eisenhower, meanwhile, is allowed a measure of dignity, presumably because he insists that the astronauts should be test pilots, not surfers, acrobats, stockcar racers or worse ('The first American in space is not going to be a chimpanzee!').

If the sections of the film concerning Yeager can be styled 'retrospective' or simply 'mythic', Kaufman's portrayal of the space race is historical revisionism, the mockery informed by the counter-culture and national disillusionment of the 60s and 70s. In place of Hawks, the

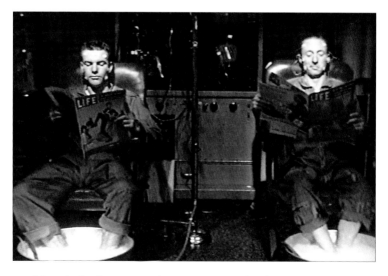

model might be the caustic, chaotic cynicism of Robert Altman – screwball gone sour, Lyndon Johnson's speech about 'controlling the high ground of space', quoted virtually word for word in this scene, sounds absurd twenty-five years into the space age (even if Reagan made

Dennis Quaid as Gordo Cooper (left)

startlingly similar pronouncements about the SDI 'Star Wars' project in the early 80s). The government instigation of a 'quick and dirty' space programme is played entirely for laughs. Jeff Goldblum (who had appeared in *Nashville* as well as Kaufman's *Invasion of the Bodysnatchers*) and Harry Shearer (best known for *This Is Spinal Tap*), the anonymous civil servants who are sent to recruit astronauts, are an out-and-out comedy duo. One tall, one short, they finish each other's sentences, but neither is capable of telling Titov from Gagarin, left from right.

Historically, the space programme can be read both as an enormously expensive, cynical exercise in Cold War *realpolitik*, and as the zenith of twentieth-century scientific utopianism. By emphasising the comedy (with variable success, it should be said) Kaufman is distancing himself from any Cold War rationale, from 'patriotism' in effect. It's a tricky balancing act, undermining Wolfe's arguably reactionary contention that whatever their real merits and accomplishments, the astronauts stood for something, they were single-combat warriors ... Cold Warriors:

We pay homage to you! You have fought back against the Russians in the heavens! There was something pure and rare about it. Patriotism! ... What the multitudes showed John Glenn and the rest ... was something else. They anointed them with the primordial tears that the right stuff commanded.[45]

Once the Cold War thaws their aura slips: 'What *was* that feeling? Why, it was the gentle slither of the mantle of soldierly glory sliding off one's shoulders... The single-combat warriors' war had been removed.'[46] Kaufman shows some of the astronauts' popularity, the press frenzy and the Glenn parade, but, contrary to Wolfe, he finds such public spectacle fraudulent, a cheapening of heroism. If *his* seven attain the right stuff, it will not be as champions or warriors; despite the hoopla, their rite of passage will be a private matter.

'Heroism and bravery are part of it, but there seems to be more to it,' Shearer tells Goldblum as they arrive at Edwards. 'They don't talk about it, that's part of the thing ...' This is the only explicit discussion of 'the right stuff' in the film, and it's inconclusive, to say the least. But this entirely fictional sequence allows those who have it – Yeager, Crossfield, Pancho – to express their scepticism about the space programme:

You boys don't need no honest-to-god pilots, what you oughta get is a little old lab rabbit to crawl up inside your damn capsule, with its heart going pitter-patter and a wire up the kazoo ... You want a pilot to be a ballistic missile ... Anybody who goes up in that damn thing is going to be spam in a can.

Despite the aces' derision, Gus, Gordo and Deke are obviously taken with the notion of becoming 'star voyagers' (emphasis on 'star'). But Kaufman sympathises more with Yeager's attitude: although John Glenn (Ed Harris) is introduced as the holder of the coast-to-coast non-stop supersonic flying record, and he's in full Marine uniform, emblazoned with medals, the context is satiric. Our first glimpse of him is on television, so he's immediately, literally, belittled. The stiff-backed Glenn looks absurd beside 'child singer' Eddie Hodges on the quiz show 'Name That Tune' (inevitably it's 'Straighten Up and Fly Right'). An anecdote about marrying his childhood sweetheart defines him as the ultimate military square. Alan Shepard (Scott Glenn) initially looks more promising, a dare-devil navy flyer with a healthy sense of humour, he signs up only when he's assured the project will be dangerous enough. But such machismo only sets him up for the worst of the humiliations and indignities the testing procedure has in store at the Lovelace Clinic.

'The Lovelace Clinic, Albuquerque, New Mexico. February, 1959'. This sequence, which lasts nearly twenty minutes, feels almost self-contained. It was filmed in an abandoned hospital in San Francisco. San Francisco and its immediate environs also stood in for Washington DC, New York, Houston, Cape Canaveral, the Australian outback ... everywhere, in fact, except Edwards air base. By shooting away from Hollywood, Kaufman was able to do things his own way, but it cost him his first production designer, Fernando Scarfioti, who said it couldn't be done and quit. Kaufman recalls:

People laughed thinking that I could find all those locations in San Francisco. We created Cape Canaveral just outside: we had Eric Sevareid, the great announcer, sitting out there at night, and off in the distance was this rocket with smoke around it, ready to blast off. But if you were to walk out there, you'd see it was a large cardboard cut-out with a wood prop holding it up.

This accounts for the shorthand the film develops, its frequent recourse to archive footage, tight framing and rapid cutting style – a visual correlative to the 'amputated language' Wolfe found among the flyers. In contrast, the occasional cutaways to Yeager and Edwards have a sense of touching base – it's somewhere grounded and real. For now, however, the astronauts are cooped up in claustrophobic, clinical environments under artificial light.

The seven are brought together at Lovelace (six of them in one smooth panning shot, as Shepard ruefully exits the first test). Unlike basic training films – *An Officer and a Gentleman*, for example – the arduous tests the candidates undergo are neither physically nor mentally 'improving', and their medical rationale is never explained. A newsreel mixes documentary footage from the time (featuring some of the real astronauts) with the actors going through their paces. According to NASA's publication *This New Ocean*:

Over thirty different laboratory tests collected chemical, encephalographic and cardiographic data ... special physiological examinations included bicycle ergometer tests, a total-body radiation count, total-body water determination, and the specific gravity of the whole body. Clinicians worked out more complete medical histories on these men than probably had ever before been attempted on human beings.[47]

Man or monkey?

The result of these tests was the elimination of just one candidate out of the thirty-two who had made it this far. Subsequent examinations included pressure-suit tests, acceleration tests, vibration tests, heat tests and loud noise tests. 'Each candidate had to prove his physical endurance on treadmills, tilt tables, with his feet in ice water, and by blowing balloons until exhausted.'[48] On screen, these bizarre and arcane procedures seem designed as a comic riposte to the astronauts' machismo. The pilots are numbered, prodded, wired, watched and psychoanalysed around the clock, all under the watchful eye of nurse Murch ( Jane Dornacker). The body is mercilessly held up for scrutiny and symbolically emasculated. When Gordo thinks he has it figured out ('The drill here is to see who can drill the brains out of nurse Murch'), she promptly presents him with a test tube for his sperm sample: 'The best results seem to be obtained through fantasisation accompanied by masturbation followed by ejaculation.' When that fails to dispel Gordo's self-confidence ('There's plenty more where that came from'), Murch insists on a meeting with his wife, from which he is pointedly excluded, though their laughter reaches his burning ears.

But the final indignity – an enema that could end in disaster at any moment – is saved for Shepard (it is described in Wolfe, right down to the exposed walk through the hospital corridors). Bravado – the self-confident assumption of heroism before the fact – can be both an attractive and a repellent quality and, characteristically, Kaufman seems to have mixed feelings about it here. He is at once indulgent and ironic: the pilots have been systematically stripped of the false trappings of heroism – their uniforms, their liberty, even their reflexes. They have stayed the course, they retain their bravado, but Lovelace has cut them down to size.

The toilet flush which climaxes the enema scene flows straight into rapturous applause at the Washington press conference on 9 April 1959. Having been under private scrutiny in the clinic, the seven are now presented for public display in a piece of phoney theatre, with stage, microphones, rows of lights. The NASA emblem and the Stars and

Stripes are much in evidence, and the astronauts are introduced with a patriotic flourish: 'Seven Americans!'

They are uneasy at first, but gain confidence as John Glenn takes control. Glenn is in the middle of the line-up, as he was historically. The conference matches Wolfe's transcription almost verbatim, though Gordo is given Glenn's line about being 'blessed' (Dennis Quaid reads it virtually tongue in cheek, a put-on for the press, whereas Ed Harris's Glenn extols family, God and country in all sincerity), and Kaufman gives Deke Slayton the *New York Times*'s line: 'We're not saying anything new here today, we're just saying the same things that need to be said again and again with fierce conviction.'

The audience laps it up, but our response is more cynical, and not just because attitudes have changed. The 'fierce conviction' of the

astronauts – Glenn aside – seems blatantly false (witness the eyebrows raised between the other six at Glenn's words). The whole show has been staged for the press, the root weevils, who are busily constructing an image of the seven which has no relation to the men we have seen. Their marriages are not particularly stable, church plays no part in their lives, and none of them has cited patriotism before now. Nor are they

The *Life* portfolio

the greatest pilots in the country, as the Air Force liaison man, Clennon, reminds us: 'Yeager should see this, seven rookies being installed as the hottest numbers in flying, and they haven't done a goddamn thing yet except show up for a press conference.' (Though even Clennon joins in the adulation before the conference is over.) Kaufman picks up the cue, cutting to Edwards air base, where Yeager and Crossfield are listening to the conference on the radio. They don't speak, but they don't look happy. The conference ends with an ironic blast from the Hallelujah Chorus which continues playing as we progress to the negotiations with *Life* magazine, which is to put the finishing touches to the astronauts' sanctification.

The press conference serves one other function: it raises the question, which of the seven will be first in space? If narratives are

The issue here is monkey

driven by conflict and resolution, then this is one of the film's few obvious motors. The focus switches to Glenn, the favourite, and the most articulate of the film's 130 speaking characters. Initially, it seems that he will be another object for counter-cultural scorn, comparable with Major Frank Burns in *M\*A\*S\*H* perhaps, adding the military to the film's institutional hit list.[49] Instead, Kaufman plays him dead straight, providing another subtle shift in our perspective on the astronauts.

'What's with her?' Trudy demands of Annie Glenn (Mary-Jo Deschanel, Caleb's wife). 'She seems snobby.' 'She's Mrs Clean Marine,' Gordo cracks. But she isn't snobby: Kaufman cuts to an intimate scene between the Glenns, sitting up together in bed, and we learn that Annie's apparent aloofness is the result of a severe stutter. After the noise and crowds of the press conference and at *Life*, this represents a chance to see the private John Glenn. It's essentially a love scene, though played out in tender glances and affectionate smiles more than in words. They discuss his imminent departure for Cape Canaveral, and Glenn's admiration for his comrades. Though he is shown to be naïve, he is allowed a measure of self-knowledge: 'I guess they think I'm kind of a gung-ho type, "Eddie Attaboy", "Harry Hairshirt" ... [Tom Wolfe's

No 'Buck Rogers', no bucks!

not-so affectionate nicknames for him]. That's me, I guess, a lonely beacon of restraint and self-sacrifice in a squall of car-crazies.' His personal ambition is tempered with a kind of philanthropy: 'It's important to America to get a man up there first. I'm planning to be the first man to ride the rocket.'

As a montage of failed launches down at Cape Canaveral makes clear, being the first to ride the rocket is not necessarily an enviable job. (Any reading of *The Right Stuff* in terms of its representation of masculinity would have a field day with this hilarious collection of phallic damp squibs and premature ejaculations; they just can't get it up.) The astronauts can do little but watch and wait. Another film might have made something romantic and heroic of the seven's experience at the Cape – there's enough talk of drinking and driving and driving and drinking in Wolfe's book. Of this we see a scene in a bar at Cocoa Beach (it's quite a bar, admittedly, with girls swimming behind a glass wall and a red filter out of *Mean Streets*). Two women enter, in all their warpaint, take in the Air Force and the Navy boys at the bar but pass on by towards Glenn and Carpenter, sitting at a table nearby. 'Four down, three to go,' they say to each other. And the camera glides up to Glenn inquiringly . . .

Glenn remains true to his principles, arguing with the rest that their womanising is putting the programme at risk. But he's fighting the wrong battle, Grissom tells him. 'The issue here ain't pussy. The issue here is monkey.' It's a typically salty Kaufman line, and a salient modification of the original dramatic question: not *who* will be first, but *what*? Because if a monkey can go into space and do an astronaut's job, where does that leave the astronauts? 'What they're trying to do is send a man up to do a monkey's work . . . us, a bunch of college-trained chimpanzees.'

A montage of training exercises illustrates the point, with first the humans, then the monkeys performing the exact same tasks (Kaufman even cuts back and forth between Glenn's pained grimace during one exercise and a monkey's identical expression in the same circumstances).[50] To the scientists, there is little enough difference between the candidates, save that the monkeys are more co-operative.

Here are the astronauts then, with their messy personal lives, their petty disputes, phoney public images and overrated flying abilities ... and the job in hand – a panicky government public relations exercise – might be performed by a monkey. Is this the stuff of heroes? On 31 January 1961, despite Eisenhower's wishes, the first American in space is Ham, a chimpanzee. And on 12 April the same year, Yuri Gagarin becomes the first human to go into orbit. Where, then, are we to find the right stuff?

In fact, Kaufman is already laying the foundations for the answer to this question. Grissom's gruff observation, midway through the film,

Donald Moffat as
Lyndon B. Johnson

that 'the issue here is monkey', is the turning-point for the seven. Henceforth, they will act as a team, use their impeccable media profile as a means of empowerment. By operating as an informal trade union, they use their *celebrity* (passive) to *heroic* (active) ends. 'No bucks, no Buck Rogers,' they explain to the scientists, insisting that the spacecraft must have a window, a hatch with explosive bolts, and pitch-and-yaw thrusters so that the astronaut can pilot its re-entry into the earth's atmosphere. 'The guinea pigs set about altering the experiment,' as

Wolfe puts it. The astronauts are bona fide mavericks now – far more sympathetic identification figures than the glorified corporate stooges we've seen so far. The competitive edge between them is transformed into friendship and loyalty, and they are rewarded with an iconic heroic image: the seven in slow motion, striding manfully abreast towards the camera through a long NASA corridor, with shafts of sunlight rippling on their shiny silver space suits and Bill Conti whipping up the score. ('They have that swagger almost like they're a gang from *The Wanderers*, about to get into a battle with a neighbouring gang, in this case the Russians – that sort of American swagger,' Kaufman says. 'For me, that's freedom without viciousness, that kind of bonding and team spirit which, within proper bounds, I really like.')

This new united front is emphasised to the point where Kaufman

Gus screws the pooch

can't bring himself to show how the astronauts themselves elect Shepard for the first flight. Instead he playfully milks the suspense until the last moment, and then immediately illustrates the moral support Shepard receives from his former rival, the favourite, Glenn. (By omitting the voting process, Shepard's selection becomes something of an anomaly within the film.) Later, when a NASA official (John Ryan) threatens to change the order of flights because Glenn has backed his (stammering) wife's refusal to meet Lyndon Johnson on live television, the other six will have no part of it. It is probably the most heroic scene in the film. Comradeship may not be the only attribute the astronauts need to share in Kaufman's radical redefinition – virtual subversion – of the right stuff, but it becomes clear that it *is* integral to it.

These scenes allow Kaufman to continue to satirise the terms on which the false prophets of the media manufacture their false gods. 'What can be going through a man's mind at this point?' asks the TV reporter, Eric Sevareid, as Alan Shepard's flight is delayed yet again, never imagining that the only thing on the astronaut's mind is his bladder (cue a series of visual puns: someone hosing down the tarmac below the rocket, endless cups of coffee as the wives watch the television broadcast at the Shepard home, the sound magnified to bursting point).

Yeager stands apart

The media circus figures large in this, the last hour of the film.
During Shepard's flight, which is over relatively quickly – less than
ninety seconds of screen time – the press corps is camped outside the
Shepard home, a menacing, alien presence akin to the zombies in
George Romero's *Night of the Living Dead*, threatening to invade the
domestic space, descending *en masse* on the only fresh meat they see, a
neighbour's laundry delivery man. Shepard returns to a hero's welcome,
cheering crowds, brass bands and a medal from President Kennedy. We
see the ceremony in black-and-white newsreel footage spliced with
degraded footage of the actors – a technique pioneered in *Citizen Kane*
and later popularised by *Forrest Gump*. It's primarily a comic, ironic
device: the better the illusion, the more we appreciate the trickery
involved (though Kaufman would explore its dramatic potential further
in *The Unbearable Lightness of Being*). In this instance, Scott Glenn was
deemed such a close physical match for his real-life counterpart that in
one shot we glimpse the back of the real Alan Shepard as Kennedy pins
on the medal.

The hollowness of all the pomp surrounding Shepard's welcome is
made apparent with the painfully different reaction to the Grissom
flight, of which we see just the splashdown. Whether, as Gus protests to
anyone who will listen, the hatch 'just blew', or whether, as the film
implies, he panicked and hit the explosive bolts (ironically, the very
feature he had won during the showdown with the capsule designers),
the Grissoms get no benefit of the doubt from NASA. There are no
crowds, no ticker-tape parades and no lunches at the White House. This
is the downside to the American Dream, the small print: if you don't
quite make the cut, you're on your own. The disappointment is
particularly bitter because, more than anyone, the Grissoms were
banking on the deal. Before the flight, Gus tells Gordo that he's taking
rolls of dimes up with him, because they'll be worth so much more after
they've been in space (an alchemy he also predicts for his sexual allure).
'You've got to think ahead . . .' he says. But fame, money, sex, these
dreams are banished now. In her very first scene, we heard Betty telling

Trudy and Marge that the military 'owed' her, how she expected them to pay. Now she repeats herself: 'The military promised, now they're welching ... Are these the goodies? Is this how the military pays off?' (The real Gus Grissom died in Apollo 1 in 1967. His widow sued for $20 million and settled for $350,000.)

If there is a sense of a cruel yet poetic justice at work here – a harsh lesson the Grissoms must learn – Kaufman nevertheless orchestrates sympathy for them: the brave face they put on for the press, Betty's whispered declaration of love and, not least, Yeager's own citation, all serve to rehabilitate Gus to the point where, at the end, he too may share in the right stuff (unthinkable in Wolfe's original terms). Yeager's view is vital, of course, because Kaufman has positioned him as the ultimate arbiter. His colleagues at Edwards are full of scorn – 'Gus screwed the pooch,' scoffs Ridley. But Yeager speaks up for his old Air Force comrade:

Think a monkey knows he's sitting on top of a rocket that might explode? These astronauts, they know that, see? Takes a special kind of man to volunteer for a suicide mission, especially one that's on TV. Old Gus did all right.

On the face of it, this simply reasserts the principle of blind courage, the crudest reading of the right stuff, but the scene refers back to a sequence immediately after the chimpanzee flight, which invited similar contempt at Edwards. Yeager appears to join in the general laughter, but later stumbles out of Pancho's and stares up at the full moon. Behind him, the men are singing 'Wild Blue Yonder', a horse snorts in the darkness ... and we understand that the cowboy pioneer heritage, passed on to the aviators in the first half of the century, is now the remit of the astronauts, the 'star voyagers'.

'Those who came before us made certain this country rode the first wave of the industrial revolution, the first wave of modern invention, and the first wave of nuclear power ... this generation does not intend to founder in the backwater in the coming age of space.' John Kennedy's words echo over the Mojave Desert, apparently consigning the Air Force base to history as Pancho's Inn is engulfed in flames. Yeager rides up to examine the charred remains and he might be in a Western ghost town. It is the end of an era. Again, Yeager is virtually silent, but Glennis joins him and does the talking for him. The mood is elegiac, but the message is salutary – we must make our terms with the present:

You know, I always hated flying ... The government spends all that time and money teaching you how to be fearless, but they don't spend a goddamn penny teaching you how to be the fearless wife of a test pilot. But I guess I liked it. I guess I liked the kind of man who could push the outside of the envelope ... But I never could stand a man who was one of those

The Yeagers back at Pancho's Fly Inn

Ed Harris as Scott Glenn

'remember-whens?', those bitter guys that just sit around talking about old times. If I ever see that happening I'm going right out the front door and you'll never catch me.

If *The Right Stuff* establishes a dialectic with the Western in its concern with 'the new frontier', masculine autonomy and its ambivalence towards modernity (science, government, the media, capitalism), the film doesn't, in the end, pertain to the narrative strategies of that genre, nor any other. The last hour comprises the four space flights and Yeager's return to the skies, and contrasts the responses on the ground. Kaufman has all but dispensed with conventional conflict/resolution narrative by this point: 'Structurally, well, it certainly didn't follow any structure that I knew of,' he recalls. In this sense, *The Right Stuff* is a deeply unAmerican movie.

As William Goldman perceived it, Glenn represents the obvious climax for a heroic movie about the astronauts: Glenn was the most gung-ho of the group and his orbit put the US back on something approaching equal terms with the Soviets, inspired national euphoria, and contained the built-in suspense of a faulty heat shield and a relatively untested rocket. In fact, the Glenn orbit does represent a kind of climax to the film, but not in the closed sense that Goldman conceived of it. Certainly Kaufman privileges Glenn: where Shepard's flight was over in ninety seconds and Grissom's in less than half a minute, the Glenn orbit merits fifteen minutes of screen time – and that after a considerable build-up including the postponed launch and Annie Glenn's refusal to see the comically apoplectic LBJ ('Isn't there anyone who can deal with a housewife?'). It is the most sustained sequence in the second half of the film. We see ground control at the Cape, the wives at home watching on television, thousands looking at news screens in New York, and Gordo with a group of Aborigines at a monitoring station in Australia. But the principal focus is on Glenn and what he sees. As in the Shepard and Grissom flights, Kaufman allows himself just a couple of basic camera set-ups within the claustrophobic confines of the capsule – a close-up of the astronaut at helmet level, and another shot from knee-height, looking up at him with a reflection of his view played out on a glass panel on his chest. In both these set-ups the colourful lights on the control panel are visible as delicate rainbow reflections running down the helmet visor, just below each eye. These 'astro tears', as the film crew called them, bestow a beguiling expression of wonderment and melancholy on the astronaut's encased face.

With Glenn's flight we also see, for the first time, exteriors of the capsule floating in outer space, a small and fragile object against vast cosmic panoramas of black, white and blue. The effect is unexpectedly liberating. Unlike the noise and judder of the test flights through the upper atmosphere, or the jolting re-entry experienced by Grissom and Shepard, the orbit is smooth and silent. Here, motion-control special effects were preferred to convey the sensation of zero gravity. They are augmented by limpid, intense evocations of space, the earth, the clouds, the sun and the moon, created by experimental film-maker Jordan Belson. Kaufman has given us glimpses of such visions before, most notably during Yeager's flight beyond Mach 2, but this time we are invited to contemplate their richness at length in a sublime, spiritual spectacle which Kaufman scores with a suite composed by Henry Mancini for *The White Dawn* – the theme derived from an Eskimo chant[51] – and, appropriately, Gustav Holst's 'The Planets'.

*The Right Stuff* has drawn on Hawks and the Western, on Altman, the New Wave and screwball traditions, but Jordan Belson belongs firmly to the avant-garde. A film-maker since the 50s, he has directed a series of abstract 16mm shorts such as *Music of the Spheres*, *Phenomena* and *Samadhi*, explorations of light and colour created in his San Francisco studio. Although some of his work was used in *Journey to the Far Side of the Sun* and Donald Cammell's *Demon Seed* (and it is rumoured that he influenced *2001*), this was the first time he had produced footage specifically for a feature, and the first time he had used 35mm. His techniques are a secret, though we know that he doesn't use animation, liquids or models, but creates real-time colour optical effects with hand-made mechanical contraptions (another instance of the pragmatic, 'jerryrigged' approach Kaufman settled on). Belson's work takes *The Right Stuff* on to an altogether higher level, one that transcends representational photography – this is something more mysterious and visionary. Colours, shapes and forms bend and melt into abstract nebulae, ethereal cinematic epiphanies.

Whereas in *2001* the characters remained impervious to the spectacle of space, barely giving it a second glance, our response here is mediated by a receptive on-screen figure: 'Oh! That view is tremendous!'. Ed Harris's Glenn says the same things Tom Wolfe's Glenn said – the same things that John Glenn actually said on 20 February 1962 – but the interpretation is very different. For Wolfe, space was anti-climactic. In conditioning out fear, the astronauts' training had conditioned out everything else with it. On Shepard's flight: 'He was introducing the era of pre-created experience. His launching was an utterly novel event in American history, and yet he could feel none of its novelty ... *he didn't feel anything at all!*'[52] On Glenn's: 'He knew every sensation he would feel once the event began ... No man had ever lived an event so completely ahead of time ... Even the view had been simulated ... Awe seemed to be demanded, but how could he express awe honestly? He had lived it all before the event.'[53]

Wolfe's account may be true to Glenn's experience – only Glenn could know – though it runs counter to the testimony of many astronauts who have subsequently gone into space and been profoundly affected by what they have seen. It *is* true of the public experience of the Apollo missions, much fresher in Wolfe's mind when he came to write *The Right Stuff*. Space lost its magical aura sometime in the wake of the moon landing in July 1969. After a decade which dared to dream about a man on the moon, the reality soon seemed, somehow, mundane. Space was just an awful lot of nothing, after all. TV audiences switched off, astronauts were reduced to doing publicity stunts (Alan Shepard golfing on the moon) and that much-anticipated brave new future, the space age, looked like a thing of the past. Its banal bequest: Velcro, Mylar, Dacron and Teflon. In *Of a Fire on the Moon*, Norman Mailer

Orbiting the earth

blamed NASA's technocratic mindset: if only the astronauts had been poets, not putters ... if only *he* had been sent up to take that giant leap, to convey the primordial blast of 'humankind touching the source of sea tides and lunacy'! Kaufman sought to restore nothing less than the promise and possibility of space. He demanded awe, and Jordan Belson sees that we get it.

The episode with the 'fireflies' that John Glenn spots around his capsule, a hundred miles above the earth, is an even clearer example of the difference between the rationalism of the book and the mysticism of the film. Again, the words are the same: 'I'll try to describe what I'm in here. I am in a big mass of some very small particles that are brilliantly lit up like they're luminescent. I never saw anything like it.' But while Wolfe reports Glenn's excitement and NASA's apparent lack of interest without comment, Kaufman dramatises the episode so that we are invited to choose between two possible explanations. On the one hand, the particles could be related to the faulty heat shield – a rational, scientific explanation which unfortunately doesn't appear to hold water (Glenn says they're independent of the capsule). On the other hand – and the movie appears to endorse this interpretation – they could emanate from the Aboriginal creation dance played out in homage to the space travellers in front of Gordo Cooper. 'That old bloke over there, he know the moon, he know the star and he know the Milky Way,' one of the Aborigines (David Gulpilil) tells Cooper, bridging thousands of years of consciousness. Kaufman dissolves from the flying embers of their bonfire to the particles swirling around Glenn, and leaves the miraculous very much a possibility.[54]

The 'fireflies' are a precursor to Glenn's fiery re-entry, a suspenseful sequence of infernal, raging reds licking at the plummeting capsule. The descent climaxes in a shock cut to the Stars and Stripes; the soundtrack cuts from the astronaut humming a defiant 'Battle Hymn of the Republic' to a full marching band rendition. Glenn's ticker-tape parade through New York (seamlessly integrating close-ups of the actors with long shots culled from colour newsreel footage) is a moment of triumph, but over in a trice, a mere historical footnote to the cathartic experience of the orbit itself. This time, Kaufman cuts mischievously from a newsreel shot of a banner proclaiming 'Hats off to the real skyscrapers' to the NF-104 rocket plane arriving at Edwards Air Force Base, and to Yeager.

Yeager is psyching out the gleaming silver plane as he did the X-1 before it. 'This is the one we've been waiting for,' Clennon observes. 'The bad news is the entire programme is probably going to be scrapped. From now on the astronaut boys in Houston have got the only ticket. Barring, of course, some unforeseen event . . .'. As Yeager walks around the plane, familiarising himself with its contours, Kaufman tracks into the gaping black rocket fuselage at its rear. As the screen becomes engulfed in black, a whistle blows and a light emerges at the end of the tunnel, for now we are coming into the Houston Coliseum as Texas welcomes its famous new arrivals, NASA's Mercury Seven.

Parallel editing highlights either contrasts or comparisons. The cross-cutting between Edwards and Houston does both. First, the contrasts: a couple of men standing quietly in relief against an open, isolated stretch of desert – the most arid and colourless of terrains – as opposed to the loud, bright razzamatazz and cheering crowds at the Coliseum, an enclosed, artificial space where LBJ himself presides as master of ceremonies. Houston represents the nadir of the phoney celebration of America constructed around the seven by the expediencies of the Cold War. There are whole carcases roasting on spits, and businessmen are buzzing like flies around Glenn in particular. Gordo Cooper acknowledges its excess in an aside to Grissom: 'Here I am, earning $20,000 a year from a magazine contract, I've got a free house and all the furnishings, got me a Corvette and a free lunch from one end of America to the other, and I haven't even been up there yet.'

The press corps approach Gordo with a question. 'Who was the best pilot I ever saw?' He laughs, looking across to Trudy, but answers soberly, with a maturity we haven't seen before, and for a few moments the glitz and the hubbub fade away as one man bears witness:

(Overleaf) Astro tears as Glenn spies 'fireflies'

Well, I'll tell you, I've seen a lot of 'em, and most of them are just pictures on a wall back at some place that doesn't even exist any more. And some of them are right here in this room [*he lays a hand on Gus*]. Some of 'em are still out there somewhere, doin' what they always do, going up each day in a hurlin' piece of machinery, putting their hides on the line, hanging it out over the edge, pushing back the outside of the envelope and hauling it back in. But there was one pilot I once saw who I think truly did have the right –

He's interrupted here by an impatient question, and changes tack, reverting to the wisecracking Gordo with his wide-boy grin the journalists prefer. 'Who was the best pilot I ever saw? Well, you're looking at him!' This crucial speech reasserts the bond between the astronauts and the pilots, illustrating the discrepancy between personal respect and public rhetoric, heroism and celebrity. It also reveals Gordo's own growth and signals his readiness to take on the mantle of the right stuff.

Back at Edwards, the camera pans up Yeager's shiny silver flight suit – at least halfway to the space suit the astronauts wear. 'Hey Ridley, you got any Beemans?' His words echo across the hangar and the wind blows across his hair. 'I think I see a plane over here with my name on it.' This is an unscheduled and unofficial flight. Solo. Yeager is out to break the Russian air-speed record, and to revitalise the Air Force rocket plane project. A cutaway to Glennis back in the empty shell of Pancho's hints at another reason too. He wants to prove he's still got it – and, perhaps, he wants to see what the star voyagers have seen.

As Yeager breaks through the clouds we cut back to the Coliseum, the stage curtains opening to reveal Miss Sally Rand, demurely naked behind two huge feather fans. (This performance is noted but briefly by Wolfe, who ungallantly points out that in 1962 the famous stripper was some decades past her peak.) Rand's 'artistic' routine to a saccharine symphonic arrangement of Debussy's 'Clair de Lune' is the very apotheosis of kitsch – and yet this is the film's most sublime sequence, the point at which *The Right Stuff* unmistakably annoints the Seven. Kaufman has related this scene to the shamanist rituals in *The White*

*Dawn* but it refers most immediately to the Aboriginal dance performed before Gordo during Glenn's flight. Caleb Deschanel shoots it so that Rand seems to be dancing on the horizon, the stage is the edge of the world and, behind her, the backdrop sky blue. The performer is silhouetted, as if by the rising sun, and her fans might be the wings of Icarus. Seated beside their wives in the darkness, the seven are also backlit – Deschanel gives each a faint golden halo. Sitting there, the blue half-light dancing across their features, they might be reflections of the movie audience watching the screen. And then, as if telepathically, they look away and to each other. Nods and half-smiles ... their fraternity is a million miles away from here in some other, private place.

Back to Yeager, turning to the sun, thrusting through Jordan Belson's 'demon zone'. At the top of the earth's atmosphere the sky turns black and Yeager is afforded a glimpse of the stars before – 'Christ Almighty!' – the NF-104 goes into vertiginous freefall, spiralling head over tail down towards the earth. When he ejects, the silence seems to consign him to the dust. He's a puny figure, dropping from the camera's view, struggling vainly with his helmet, until he's lost to our eyes as well as our ears, swallowed by the clouds below.

Clouds which are also ostrich feathers, borne by Sally Rand in the Houston Coliseum. Again Kaufman cuts between the seven. This time the music fades, and the astronauts look up, their antennae picking up the explosion of Yeager's crashed plane in the high California desert. This then is their connection with Yeager, the kinship they may claim: to dream of flight and face down death – that takes the right stuff.

The black smoke is like a scar in the sky. An ambulance emerges through the heat haze and the driver thinks he spots something moving in the distance. 'Sir, over there – is that a man?'

Ridley looks across and sees the sun flashing off a silver suit. 'Yeah, you're darn right it is.' The music swells and there is Yeager, striding across the sand, helmet in one hand, parachute in the other.[55] One half of his face is charred but his jaw is set in bloodied determination. Like Glenn, he has defied death to snatch a glimpse of the heavens. This will

Yeager in the upper atmosphere

Feathers like the wings of Icarus

Falling without end

Is that a man?

be our last look at Yeager, and it's among the most transcendent images in contemporary cinema: 'A lonely figure in a pressure suit walking across the face of a planet – it could be a moon, any moon at all. And he walks on and on.' (Not Wolfe, but Kaufman's screenplay.)

*Is that a man? You're darn right it is.* The director dares to undercut even this brave assertion. A date caption relays us to 15 May 1963, where the very flawed, very human Gordo Cooper lies fast asleep in the space capsule prior to his 'suicide mission'. Seagulls wheel outside his craft. After a textbook launch, egged on by Gus Grissom, John Glenn and even the press ('Go, go, go'), Gordo has his first glimpse of outer space, and a film that began with the spectre of death, the demon that lives in the air, ends on an ear-to-ear grin and a note of spiritual grace: 'The sun is coming through the window now. Oh Lord, what a heavenly light!'

## 5 Epilogue: 1983

When *The Right Stuff* was released in October 1983, it was a Ladd Company production, distributed through Warner Bros. Faced with the disastrously expensive *Heaven's Gate* (which had been released in 1980 and written off to the tune of $40 million) UA promptly dropped the space epic, and in fact the studio was sold soon afterwards. Armed with a complete storyboard, and having embarked on what would be a massive trawl through stock footage, Kaufman, Chartoff and Winkler convinced the Ladd Company they could do the movie for a budget of $10.5 million below the line, though the final budget was closer to the $20 million UA had originally estimated (Kaufman claims $19 million, while other sources go as high as $27 million).

The first press preview was a rough-cut screening for *Newsweek*, which ran a cover story about how the film might influence the presidential prospects of Senator John Glenn who was then campaigning against Walter Mondale for the Democratic ticket. *Newsweek* critic David Ansen raved about the film. 'An American epic, a movie with all the Right Stuff.' His colleagues followed suit. Richard Schickel: 'A grand, yet edifying entertainment.' Roger Ebert: 'It is in the great tradition of such intelligent American epics as *The Godfather*, *Chinatown*, *Nashville* and *Apocalypse Now*.' Gene Siskel: 'It's a great film, obviously. A very important film historically.' Judith Crist: 'A magnificent movie. The epic of the year, a grand and glorious entertainment.'

Almost all the reviews made reference to the Glenn campaign and, interestingly in the light of the debate with Goldman, many critics found Kaufman was more sympathetic to the astronauts than Wolfe had been, although a couple of them, Marcia Pally in *Film Comment* and Pauline Kael in the *New Yorker*, bridled at double standards and sleight of hand in the transition from satire to celebration. 'Being far more of an anti-authoritarian than Tom Wolfe, Kaufman probably felt he had transformed the material, but he is still stuck with its reactionary cornerstone: the notion that a man's value is determined by his physical courage,' wrote Kael. Nevertheless she concluded: 'The movie has the happy, excited spirit of a fanfare, and it's astonishingly entertaining, considering what a screw-up it is ... a stirring, enjoyable mess of a movie.'[56]

'Across the board appeal to all spectrums and looks to do strong, sustained biz,' opined *Variety*, deciding that the time was right for *The Right Stuff*. 'A somewhat revived sense of patriotism and awareness of things military over the past three years, and even the return of short haircuts and a "clean" look for men ... Just a few years ago, getting gung-ho about *The Right Stuff* couldn't have been possible for young hipsters.'[57] The industry publication *Motion Picture Digest* summed up the general euphoria with a rhetorical flourish: 'How can it miss at the box-office?'[58]

*The Right Stuff* took a disappointing $21.5 million in North American receipts. 'When the trailer played in San Francisco it was booed by people because they felt it was too patriotic,' recalls Kaufman. The movie's messages may have been too mixed for a mass audience; the length, historical subject matter and reverential 'event-film' marketing may have proved intimidating.

They released it in something like five theatres, it was what they called 'platforming'. Warner Bros had at one point offered the Ladd company a thousand theatres at Christmas-time, which was leading into the modern concept of releasing, but Laddie [Alan Ladd Jr] really wanted an October release built around a premiere at the Kennedy Centre ... There was a huge party, with Walter Cronkite and all the press, Gordo Cooper, Schirra, Carpenter and Slayton ... Kissinger was there. I cranked the sound right up. I said if you can see Kissinger's sleeves fluttering on the launches then the sound is high enough. The next day there was supposed to be this fly-by, led by Chuck Yeager, the entire history of aircraft, followed, they hoped, by the space shuttle flying over the Potomac, which would be lined by a million people. Incredible publicity ...

The parade goes by

Cut to us on the roof of the Kennedy Centre. There's a bunch of people from the press up there, and someone says 'There they are!' I look up and there are three airplanes way off in the distance – they couldn't get access through the Washington flight patterns. I looked down at the Potomac River, and there was one guy with a fishing pole down there, and I knew we were in trouble ... I've often wondered if it had been released fifteen years later what fate it might have had.

In the UK, the critics were divided. Some complained the movie was too patriotic, too macho, or simply too long. Others recognised a modern American masterpiece. In Paris, *The Right Stuff* played for over a year. Nominated for eight Academy Awards, including best picture, cinematography and supporting actor (Sam Shepard), *The Right Stuff* won four: best original score, editing, sound and sound editing.

John Glenn lost the Democratic nomination to Walter Mondale, who went on to lose the 1984 presidential election to Ronald Reagan. Philip Kaufman did not make another film until *The Unbearable Lightness of Being* in 1987.

# Notes

**1** Quoted in Bill Krohn, 'La Légende des Pionniers du Cosmos', *Cahiers du Cinéma*, April 1984.

**2** Tom Wolfe, *The Right Stuff* (London: Picador, 1991), p. 67.

**3** *Mercury Project Summary* (NASA, 1963).

**4** Ibid.

**5** Cited in Wolfe, *The Right Stuff*, p. 107.

**6** Tom Wolfe, *The New Journalism* (London: Picador, 1990), p. 15.

**7** Ibid., p. 28.

**8** Ibid., p. 35.

**9** Wolfe, *The Right Stuff*, p. 9.

**10** Ron Reagan, *Interview*, July 1983.

**11** Wolfe, *The Right Stuff*, p. 29.

**12** Steven Bach, *Final Cut: Dreams and Disaster in the Making of 'Heaven's Gate'*, 2nd rev. edn (London: Pimlico, 1996), pp. 309–10.

**13** Ibid., p. 311.

**14** William Goldman, *Adventures in the Screen Trade: A Personal View of Hollywood and Screenwriting*, (London: Futura, 1985), p. 254.

**15** Ibid., p. 255.

**16** ibid., p. 257.

**17** Stephen Farber, *Film Comment*, Jan./Feb. 1979.

**18** *American Film*, November 1983.

**19** 'We've deliberately set this in 1963, the year that Kennedy was assassinated,' Kaufman said of *The Wanderers*. 'From World War II until about '63, there was an isolated macho world that guys could operate in . . . [It was] the last year of white gangs. Bob Dylan was coming in, and the Beatles were about to land, drugs were about to break loose. Kids were about to hear other voices . . . They were about to hear that they must take part in a larger world.' *Film Comment*, Jan./Feb. 1979. 1963 was also the year that Phil Kaufman became a film-maker.

**20** Kaufman's films since *The Right Stuff* are all adaptations, and two of them are historical: *The Unbearable Lightness of Being* (1987); *Henry and June* (1990); and *Rising Sun* (1993). In 1995 he was executive producer on the TV documentary *China: The Wild East*.

**21** *Film Comment*, Jan./Feb. 1979.

**22** Goldman, *Adventures in the Screen Trade*, p. 257.

**23** Wolfe, *The Right Stuff*, p. 29.

**24** Goldman, *Adventures in the Screen Trade*, p. 259.

**25** Bach, *Final Cut*, p. 344.

**26** Goldman, *Adventures in the Screen Trade*, p. 258.

**27** The Apollo programme consumed an astonishing $24 billion, or 25 per cent of the US Federal budget throughout the 60s. At its peak, it cost 50 cents every week for every man, woman and child in America.

**28** *Cahiers du Cinéma*, April 1984.

**29** Goldman, *Adventures in the Screen Trade*, p. 260.

**30** Goldman suggests that six pages of his original 148-page screenplay survived, 'a bitter fight between an astronaut and his wife'. Again, Kaufman queries this. The scene – between the Grissoms – sticks closely to Tom Wolfe.

**31** A late replacement for John Barry, Conti won the Academy Award for his score, though both he and Kaufman have voiced dissatisfaction with it.

**32** The opening shot of *Invasion of the Bodysnatchers*, after the space pre-credit sequence, is virtually identical.

**33** In the book, Tom Wolfe claims that the reason all American pilots talk with an unflappable West Virginia drawl is directly attributable to the influence of Yeager. Wolfe, *The Right Stuff*, p. 45.

**34** David Thomson, *The Movies*, July 1983. See also Thomson on Sam Shepard, *Film Comment*, Nov./Dec. 1983.

**35** Wolfe, *The Right Stuff*, p. 47.

**36** *Film Comment*, Jan./Feb. 1979.

**37** *LA Times*, 22 January 1984.

**38** *Film Comment*, Nov./Dec. 1983.

**39** Sam Shepard, *Falling Without End*.

**40** Is it a coincidence that this joke mimics Robert Redford's meeting with Katharine Ross in *Butch Cassidy and the Sundance Kid*?

**41** For a detailed discussion of the special effects in the film, see Adam Eisenberg in *Cinefex*, October 1983.

**42** Kaufman only develops those four astronauts whose missions we are to see. Slayton never went up and his presence at Edwards is therefore not particularly helpful. Grissom's orbit was always essential: he 'screwed the pooch', a vital dramatic counterpoint to the successful missions. Kaufman won't have time for Schirra's textbook orbit, nor Carpenter's experimentation in space, but unlike Goldman, he will climax with Cooper, not the more obvious Glenn.

**43** Kaufman: 'We tried radishes, but they didn't work at all.'

**44** In fact the Soviets were not installed at Star City in 1957.

**45** Wolfe, *The Right Stuff*, p. 291.

**46** Ibid., p. 364.

**47** Lloyd Swenson Jr, James Grimwood, Charles Alexander, *This New Ocean* (NASA, 1966).

**48** Ibid.

**49** In fact, NASA, the Air Force and the US Navy all co-operated in the production of *The Right Stuff*.

**50** This sequence climaxes the first half of the two-part TV edition of the film.

**51** In James Houston's novel, *The White Dawn*, the chant is in imitation of the flight of seagulls: 'Ayii, ayii, ayii/My arms, they wave high in the air/My hands, they flutter behind my back/They wave above my head/Like the wings of a bird.'

**52** Wolfe, *The Right Stuff*, p. 218.

**53** Ibid., p. 269.

**54** 'There's science, and then there's where science has not yet gone. That isn't in Wolfe. I guess that came from saying too many mantras,' Kaufman jokes. Rationalists may like to know that NASA eventually determined that the particles were in fact ice crystals.

**55** Roland Emmerich appropriated this in *Independence Day*.

**56** *New Yorker*, 17 October 1983.

**57** *Variety*, 12 October 1983.

**58** *Motion Picture Product Digest*, vol. 11, no. 9.2, November 1983.

# Credits

**THE RIGHT STUFF**

**USA**
1983

**Production Company**
The Ladd Company
A Robert Chartoff-Irwin
Winkler production
A Philip Kaufman film
A Ladd Company release
thru Warner Bros.
**Executive Producer**
James D. Brubaker
**Producers**
Irwin Winkler, Robert Chartoff
**Production Co-ordinator**
Jo Ann May-Pavey
**Production Manager**
James D. Brubaker
**Unit Production Managers**
David Whorf
Additional Unit:
Ned Kopp
Desert/Aerial Unit:
Larry Powell
**Location Manager**
Michael Polaire
**Assistant Production**
**Administrator**
Christine Whitney
**Additional Locations**
Stephen S. Benseman,
Patrick Ranahan, Rory Enke
**Production Accountants**
Art Schaefer
Assistant:
Lynne Birdt
**Assistant to Mr. Chartoff**
Lori Sussman
**Assistant to Mr. Winkler**
Janet Crosby
**Production Assistants**
Joey Dacow, Kevin Breslin,
Jonathan Fairbanks,
Robert Evans Lowy

**Production Secretaries**
Diane Jackson,
Susan Roether, Diana Wells
**Director**
Philip Kaufman
**First Assistant Directors**
Charles A. Myers
Additional Unit:
Charles A. Myers
Desert/Aerial Unit:
Edward F. Milkovich
**Second Assistant**
**Directors**
L. Dean Jones Jr
Additional:
Sharon Mann,
Michael Looney
Additional Unit:
Nancy Giebink
**Assistants to Mr. Kaufman**
Barbara Parker, Peter
Kaufman, Karen Frerichs
**Script Supervisor**
Alice Tompkins
**Casting**
Lynn Stalmaster, Toni Howard
& Associates
Assistants:
Patricia de Oliveira,
Gail Eisenstadt
Extra:
Northern California Casting
San Francisco Additional:
Ann Brebner
**Crowd Promotion**
**Co-ordinator**
Christine Claycombe-Brooks
**Promotion Consultant**
Dale Benson
**Screenplay**
Philip Kaufman
Based on the book by Tom
Wolfe; a four part article on
the astronauts by Tom Wolfe
originally appeared in Rolling
Stone, 1973
**Director of Photography**
Caleb Deschanel

**Camera Operators**
Craig Denault
Additional:
Ray De La Motte, Hiro Narita,
Ned McClean
**First Assistant**
**Cameraman**
Alan Disler
**Second Assistant**
**Cameraman**
Christopher Squires
**Desert Assistant**
**Cameraman**
Jeffrey Gershman
**Aerial Photography**
Clay Lacy Aviation,
Tallmantz Aviation, Art Scholl,
Jim Beebe
**Steadicam Operators**
Harry Mathias, Ted Churchill
**Key Grip**
Jonathan Guterres
**Grip Best Boys**
Dennis Pope,
Hugh C. Byrne Jr
**Grips**
Gary M. Brickley, Steven L.
Cardellini. Girard A. Gill Jr,
Thomas Sindicich
**Supervising Gaffer**
Gary Holt
**Gaffer**
Jeffrey Gilliam
**Best Boy**
Stephen J. Gardner
**Electricians**
Maurice Beesley,
David O. Childers,
Brad L. Jerrell, Medel Ramos
**Greensman**
Alan Covey Jr
**Video**
Technician:
Louis E. Mahler
Operator:
Paul Jay Murphy
Assistant:
Elizabeth Bailey

**Special Visual Creations**
Jordan Belson
**Special Photographic Effects**
USFX/Colossal Pictures
**Special Visual Effects**
Supervisor:
Gary Gutierrez
Production Manager:
Whitney Green
Production Administrator:
Richard Kerrigan
Effects Cameramen:
John V. Fante, Rick Fichter,
William Neil, Donald Dow,
Michael Lawler, Stewart
Barbee, Karl Hermmann
First Assistant Cameramen:
Martin Rosenberg, Patrick
Turner, Peter Daulton
Second Assistant
Cameramen:
Deborah Morgan,
Toby Heindel, William
Groshelle, Gregory Kimble
Key Grips:
Michael Bottero,
Peter Hadres, Dan Kuhn,
Chris Strohmeyer
Art Supervisor:
Jena Holman
Art Assistant:
Kris Boxwell
Chief Stage Technicians:
Jan M. Heyneker,
Jay Ignaszewski
**Process Supervisor**
Lawrence G. Robinson
**Process Co-ordinators**
Donald R. Hansard,
William G. Hansard Jr
**Additional Opticals**
Cinematte Company,
Du Art Film Lab, Pacific Title
**Special Effects**
Supervisor:
Kenneth Pepiot
Foremen:
Stan Parks, David Pier
**Pyrotechnician**
Thaine Morris

**Chief Model Designers**
Frank Morelli, Mark Stetson
**Model Shop Supervisor**
Earle Murphy
**Modelmakers**
Bill Buttfield, David Carothers
Peter Kleinow, Bruce
Richardson, Tom Rudduck,
David Shwartz,
Zuzana Swansea
**Motion Control Systems Designer**
Zac Bogart
**Mechanical Designer**
Rick Perkins
**Technical Researcher**
Gary Platek
**Technical Engineering Adviser**
Rod P. Sharpe
**Technical Assistance**
Rockwell International
Corporation
**Engineering Consultant**
Gordon Stout
**Computer Programmer**
Jon Rynn
**Photographic Printer**
H. Kent Hendricks
**Editors**
Glenn Farr, Lisa Fruchtman,
Stephen A. Rotter, Tom Rolf,
Douglas Stewart
**Editorial Consultant**
John Teton
**Editorial Co-ordinators**
Terry Lynn Allen, Peter
Amundson, Leigh Blicher,
Diana Pellegrini
**First Assistant Editors**
Louis Benioff,
Victor Livingston
**Assistant Editors**
Sara Roberts, Jennifer
Weyman-Cockle, Jeff Watts
**Apprentice Editors**
Clifford Latimer, Bob Sarles,
Franklin Simeone,
David Dresher, John Morris,
Susanna Blaustein,
Robert Yano

**Editorial Assistant**
Nicole Boris
**Editorial Apprentice**
Jenny Oznowicz
**Production Designer**
Geoffrey Kirkland
**Visual Consultant**
Gene Rudolf
**Art Directors**
Richard J. Lawrence,
W. Stewart Campbell,
Peter Romero
**Set Designers**
Craig Edgar, Joel David
Lawrence, Nicanor Navarro
**Set Decorators**
Pat Pending,
George R. Nelson
**Storyboards**
Gary Gutierrez, Tim Boxell,
Richard Larson
**Set Dressers**
Lead:
George Ziminsky,
Thomas J. Furginson,
Peteris M. Bankins
Additional:
Steve Banks,
Donald E. Kerns
**Supervising Construction Co-ordinator**
Cal DiValerio
**Construction Co-ordinator**
Dwight E. Williams
Construction Foremen
Bruce DiValerio, Leo Loverro,
James Doyle Schwalm
**Paint Co-ordinator**
Elizabeth Hamilton
**Paint Foreman**
Dale Halgo
**Standby Painter**
Robert Evans
**Labour Foreman**
Thomas Anderson
**Supervising Property Master**
Emily Ferry

**Property Masters**
Paul Dal Porto
Assistant:
James R. Allen
**Costume Supervisor**
Jim Tyson
**Women's Costumer**
Winnie Brown
**Costumers**
William Browder, Jill Maley,
John Napolitano
**Promotion Wardrobe
Co-ordinator**
Monique Montgomery
**Drapery**
Supervisor:
Don Watson
Foreman:
Dale Edward Cowart
**Make-up Artists**
J. Yvonne Curry,
Karen Bradley
**Hairstylists**
Bruce Geller, Patricia Grover,
Catherine Childers
**Title Design**
Dan Curry
**Titles/Opticals**
Modern Film Effects
**Music**
Bill Conti
Additional:
Garth Hudson, Todd
Boekelheide
**Music Editors**
Stephen A. Hope
Source:
Susan Crutcher,
Vivien Hillgrove Gilliam
**Scoring Mixer**
Dan Wallin
**Music Research**
Forrest G. Patten
**Music Extracts**
"Southwestern Waltz" by
Vaughn Horton, performed
by Bob Wills; "Faraway
Places" by Joan Whitney,
Alex Kramer, performed by
Margaret Whiting; "I Got a
Rocket in My Pocket" by

J. Logsdon, V. McAlpin,
performed by Jimmy Lloyd;
"Wheel of Fortune" by
B. Benjamin, G.D. Weiss,
performed by Kay Starr;
"Tennessee Waltz" by Redd
Stewart, Pee Wee King,
performed by Patti Page;
"Yablochka" (trad) arranged
by Mark Selivan, performed
by The Andreyev Balalaika
Ensemble; "Good Golly Miss
Molly" by Marascalgo,
Blackwell, perfomed by Little
Richard; "La Bamba" by
Ritchie Valens, performed by
Chubby Checker; "I Only
Have Eyes for You" by Harry
Warren, performed by The
Flamingos; "The U.S. Air
Force" by Robert Crawford;
"Hallelujah Chorus" by
George Frideric Handel,
performed by The London
Philharmonic Orchestra,
conducted by Carl Richter;
"Anchors Aweigh" (trad)
arranged by Genaro Nunez,
performed by Banda Taurina;
"Stars & Stripes" performed
by The Pride of the 48th;
music from "White Dawn" by
Henry Mancini, performed by
The London Symphony
Orchestra, conducted by
Henry Mancini; main title
music from "Sorcerer"
by/performed by Tangerine
Dream; "The Distance from
Here" performed by Michael
Garrison; "Taiko Drums"
by/performed by Seiichi
Tanaka; "Mars, Jupiter &
Neptune" (from "The Planets")
by Gustav Holst, performed
by The Boston Symphony
Orchestra, conducted by
Seiji Ozawa; "The Wayward
Wind" by Stan Lebowsky,
Herb Newman, performed by
Gogi Grant

**Production Sound Mixer**
David R.B. MacMillan
**Sound Technician**
Karen Brocco
**Supervising Re-recording
Mixer**
Mark Berger
**Re-recording Mixers**
Tom Scott, Randy Thom,
Andy Wiskes,
Todd Boekelheide
Assistant:
Stephen Sutter
**Location/Sound Effects
Mixer**
David Parker
**Supervising Sound Editor**
Jay Boekelheide
**Supervising Dialogue
Editor**
Richard Hymns
**Dialogue Editors**
Barbara McBane,
Vivien Hillgrove Gilliam
Assistants:
Sandina Bailo, Michael
Silvers, Marilyn McCoppen,
Karen Spangenberg
**Sound Effects**
Editors:
Tim Holland, Pat Jackson,
John Benson, Karen Wilson
Assistants:
Sukey Fontelieu, Christopher
Weir, Michael Magill,
Tom Christopher
**Sound Apprentices**
Fred Runner, Paige Sartorius,
Jeane Putnam
**Changes Assistant**
Mary-Helen Leasman
**Boom Operator**
Stephen E. Powell
**Cableman**
Danny Benson
**ADR**
Editor:
C.J. Appel
Assistants:
Tom Bellfort, Sandina Bailo

**Foley**
Editor:
Diana Pellegrini
Artist:
Dennie Thorpe
**Transportation**
Co-ordinator
Russell McEntyre:
Captains:
Bruce Richardson,
Danny Riportella
Co-captains:
Ed Arter, Ed Wirth
**Craft Service**
Michael O'Donnell
**Unit Publicist**
Tom Gray
**Still Photography**
Ron Grover
**Technical Consultant**
Brig. Gen. Charles E.
(Chuck ) Yeager, USAF (Ret.)
**Technical Adviser**
Duncan Wilmore
**Historical Research**
Ted Bear, Dr. Richard P.
Hallion, Nancy Olexo
**Military Liaison Officers**
Lt. Col. Dave Wagner, USA;
Lt. Pixie Larson, USN;
Capt. Nancy LaLuntas,
USMC; Lt. Col. Howard
Kosters, USAF; Maj. Royce
Grones, USAF; Capt. Don
Aites, USCG; Lt. Col.
Heinrich Thueringer, German
Air Force
**Stock Footage Research**
Karen Bergman, Dell Byrne,
Larry Heflin, Gloria Borders
**Stunt Co-ordinator**
Buddy Joe Hooker
**Parachute Stunts**
Phil Pastuhov, Rande
DeLuca, Joseph Leonard
Svec, B.J. Worth
**Stunt Pilots**
Arthur Scholl, Clay Lacy
**Special Thanks to**
Wally Nicita, Walter Murch

**Sam Shepard**
Chuck Yeager
**Scott Glenn**
Alan Shepard
**Ed Harris**
John Glenn
**Dennis Quaid**
Gordon Cooper
**Fred Ward**
Gus Grissom
**Barbara Hershey**
Glennis Yeager
**Kim Stanley**
Pancho Barnes
**Veronica Cartwright**
Betty Grissom
**Pamela Reed**
Trudy Cooper
**Scott Paulin**
Deke Slayton
**Charles Frank**
Scott Carpenter
**Lance Henriksen**
Wally Schirra
**Donald Moffat**
Lyndon B. Johnson
**Levon Helm**
Jack Ridley
**Mary Jo Deschanel**
Annie Glenn
**Scott Wilson**
Scott Crossfield
**Kathy Baker**
Louise Shepard
**Mickey Crocker**
Marge Slayton
**Susan Kase**
Rene Carpenter
**Mittie Smith**
Jo Schirra
**Royal Dano**
minister
**David Clennon**
liaison man
**Jim Haynie**
Air Force major
**Jeff Goldblum**
**Harry Shearer**
recruiters
**Scott Beach**
chief scientist

**Jane Dornacker**
nurse Murch
**Anthony Munoz**
Gonzales
**John P. Ryan**
head of program
**Darryl Henriques**
Life reporter
**Eric Sevareid**
himself
**William Russ**
Slick Goodlin
**Christopher P. Beale**
**Richard Dupell**
**William Hall**
**John X. Heart**
**Ed Holmes**
**Drew Letchworth**
**Jack Bruno Tate**
the permanent press corps
**Edward Anhalt**
grand designer
**Mary Apick**
woman reporter
**Robert Beer**
Dwight D. Eisenhower
**Erik Bergmann**
Eddie Hodges
**James M. Brady**
aide to Lyndon B. Johnson
**Katherine Conklin**
woman TV reporter
**Maureen Coyne**
waitress
**Tom Dahlgren**
**John Lion**
Bell Aircraft executives
**Peggy Davis**
Sally Rand
**John Dehner**
Henry Luce
**Robert Elross**
review board president
**Drew Eshelman**
assistant scientist
**Robert J. Geary**
game show M.C.
**Major Royce Grones**
first X-1 pilot
**David Gulpilil**
aborigine

**Anthony Wallace**
Australian driver
**Kaaren Lee**
young widow
**Sandy Kronemeyer**
**Frankie Di**
Cocoa Beach girls
**Michael Pritchard**
**Ed Corbett**
Texans
**O-Lan Shepard**
pretty girl
**Mark Todd**
**Alan Gebhart**
astronaut trainees
**General Chuck Yeager**
Fred

17,334 feet
21,616 feet (70mm)
193 minutes

**Dolby stereo**
**In Colour**
Monaco-San Francisco
**Prints**
Technicolor

Credits compiled by Markku
Salmi

Yeager and a plane
with his name on it

**BFI Modern Classics** is an exciting new series
which combines careful research with high quality
writing about contemporary cinema.  Authors write
on a film of their choice, making the case for its
elevation to the status of classic.  The series will
grow into an influential and authoritative commentary
on all that is best in the cinema of our time.
If you would like to receive further information about
future **BFI Modern Classics** or about other books on
film, media and popular culture from BFI Publishing,
please fill in your name and address and return this
card to the BFI*.
No stamp needed if posted in the UK, Channel
Islands, or Isle of Man.

NAME

ADDRESS

POSTCODE

* North America: Please return your card to:
Indiana University Press, Attn: LPB, 601 N Morton Street,
Bloomington, IN 47401-3797

**BFI Publishing
21 Stephen Street
FREEPOST 7
LONDON W1E 4AN**